CONTENTS

Cover An outtake from the *Aladdin Sane* cover shoot by Brian Duffy, 1973. © Duffy Archive & The David Bowie Archive
Back cover Bowie as Ziggy Stardust, 1973. Lynn Goldsmith/Camera Press
Inside front David, Angie and Zowie Bowie in Amsterdam, 1974. Roger Bamber/News Syndication
Right Bowie in 1976, when he metamorphosed from the plastic-soul singer of *Young Americans* to the Thin White Duke of *Station to Station*. Steve Schapiro/Corbis

With thanks to Matt Brown, Thomas Calvocoressi, Isabelle Emmerich, Jeremy Farr, Amy Hanna, Denise Kelly, Sally Mitchenall, Kelly Preedy, Sara Rumens, Luke Sale, Matthew Swift, Portia Webb and Emma Woodroofe

Edited by Ed Potton

6 CAITLIN MORAN
8 THE MUSIC
14 THE LIFE
16 THE FRIENDSHIP
18 THE FILMS
20 THE FASHION
24 THE BEST SONGS
26 THE EARLY YEARS
32 SPACE ODDITY
36 ZIGGY STARDUST
44 YOUNG AMERICANS
48 THE THIN WHITE DUKE
52 THE BERLIN TRILOGY
56 LET'S DANCE
64 LIVE AID
66 TIN MACHINE
68 THE DIGITAL REBOOT
74 THE FAMILY
78 THE COMEBACK
82 THE ALBUMS
84 THE READING LIST
86 THE CONNECTIONS

C000218494

THE TIMES
BOWIE
THE DEFINITIVE GUIDE

CAITLIN MORAN ON HER HERO

As an odd, unfriended teenage girl, the writer was saved by her famous heroes. She would turn into them, and borrow bits of them while she worked out who she was. David Bowie was at the centre of her fantasy

W hat a lucky planet we were to have had David Bowie. So lucky. Imagine how vast all of space and time is – how endless and empty, how black and cold. Imagine a tracking shot across the universe, nothing happening nearly everywhere, nearly all the time.

And then, as it scrolls past our galaxy, you can hear, quiet at first, but getting louder as we close in, *Rebel Rebel*, coming from our planet, from our country, in our time, playing on tinny transistor radios, in a million bedrooms, as a whole generation, and the next, and the next, straighten their spines, and feel their pulses rise, and say: "This. This is how I feel. Or at least, this is how I feel now. Now I've heard this."

Art shows us there are two ways to parent; to pass on your essence; to live for ever. The first is to have children. The second is to create a new kind of person, to embody a change so joyous, potent, liberating and kinetic that others, in their millions, follow suit, and become parented by you, by choice.

The hypnotist Paul McKenna was on Radio 4's *Saturday Live* recently, talking about how to be confident. The secret was to think of someone who you thought of as self-possessed, and pretend to be them. Stand as they would. Act as they would. As the drag queens say: "Fake it till you make it."

McKenna's example was Sean Connery: "Just raise your eyebrow."

But for millions, for me, it was Bowie we pretended to be, whenever we were lonely or scared or full of that itchy, awful, brilliant desire to become something bigger than we were. That's what heroes are, they show us a new way to stand that gives us confidence. They change our body language. They rewire our brains. They give us permission to become other. To become bigger. To become wilder and bolder when the only way forward in your life is to become wilder, and bolder, or else you will simply not exist.

When I was growing up in a world short of female role models, Bowie was a feminist one for me. He wasn't aligned with any particular gender, or sexuality, or culture. He presented himself as a joyful alien, singing songs directly to, and for, anyone who felt weird, or lonely. As an odd, unfriended teenage girl in my bedroom, it was perfectly clear to me that David Bowie knew about me, and was trying to recruit me to be his friend. When he eulogised the hero of *Rebel Rebel* with their torn dress, and their face a mess, concluding "Hot tramp, I love you so", that was me. Likewise, in *Rock'n'Roll Suicide*, when he told me I wasn't alone and begged me to give him my hands "Cos you're wonderful", I was his muse. Whenever I

Above
Bowie as Ziggy Stardust in 1972. He knew it would be easier to create something dazzlingly, lastingly new than it would be to try to fit in

Left
Caitlin Moran assumed the guise of Bowie – as photographed in 1974 by Terry O'Neill to promote the *Diamond Dogs* album – for a 2014 *Times Magazine* feature on her heroes

am asked, "as a feminist", if I "believe" in wearing make-up, I reply, simply: "If David Bowie can wear make-up, so can I."

I've had 20 years to think about it, and I really don't think I'm projecting. As an outsider himself – a ginger, bonk-eyed, snaggle-toothed bisexual in a dress, in Bromley – Bowie was singing to everyone like him. He knew it would be easier to create something dazzlingly, grindingly, blastingly new – to take pop to the kabuki theatres of Japan, the German avant garde, into space – than it would be to try to fit in. He intended to terraform a whole new world, and take pop – and us – with him. The Beatles, similarly, created a whole new world but they were part of a gang, a self-support system. And they were heterosexual. To paraphrase the oft-repeated homily about Ginger Rogers, Bowie did everything the Beatles did, but backwards, in heels, and alone.

Bowie's velocity and daring were so astonishing and so outrageously successful that it's impossible to pick the shrapnel of his big bang out of popular culture without tearing it to bits. Everywhere pop music is bold, ambitious, odd, dressed up – whenever it looks like nothing you've ever seen before – when it's Madonna, or Gaga, or Pet Shop Boys, or Daft Punk, or Beyoncé – it is using the tools and framework largely built by one man

from Bromley with tombstone teeth, and his name borrowed from a fixed-blade knife.

And, alongside the big picture, Bowie specialised in moments: the most aching, perfect, precision moments. Has a better love lyric ever been written than the simple, "I absolutely love you" in *Absolute Beginners*? Millions have written a million more words; he did it in four.

His command "Let's dance" feels as if dancing is the most momentous, consequential thing you can do. And he is correct – sometimes, crossing a dancefloor and dancing with someone can change your life.

The vertical take-off in *Life On Mars?*, when suddenly everything changes because "the film is a saddening bore/ For she's lived it ten times or more" and then those "Sailors, fighting in the dancehall!/ Oh man, look at those cavemen go!" It is every terrifying, amazing Friday night out in a provincial town, in an era where boredom, and violence, and conformity were everywhere, and the only way out was to find a song and climb into it, and live in it, like Narnia. Like Wonderland. And then to spend the rest of your life finding others who also knew that Wonderland, who were intent on making this world more like that. David Bowie fans.

"In life, there's only one rule," the journalist Miranda Sawyer wrote on Facebook. "Don't trust

anyone who doesn't like David Bowie." It's about as certain a law to live by as any other.

Why is it sad? Why is it sad that he's gone? Why am I mourning the death of David Bowie more than any other I have known? Why does it feel as if the world is flatter, and colder, and less able to transcend than it was before? It's because an energy source has been turned off; a world-view has disappeared. We will never again see things through Bowie's eyes: a man so effortlessly able to write the songs of the human heart, to explain ourselves back to ourselves that he spent his last 18 months writing an album to tell us he was dying. He released it only three days before he passed, the song *Lazarus* plainly stating it, yet no one knew.

As the music writer Graeme Thomson put it so beautifully on Twitter: "We were so thrilled to have him back we failed to notice he was saying goodbye."

But we were lucky. We were a lucky planet, and it was a lucky time. In all the cold, silent, black emptiness of space, we were the ones who had David Bowie. And he had us. He invented something as astonishing as a currency, or a medicine, or a machine, or a circuit, or a city. He was an emotional statesman – a president of possible futures. Thank you, you beautiful man. Thank you for giving us us. ●

BOWIE **THE MUSIC**

He was both a part of us and from a distant galaxy that we had no chance of reaching

---

Brilliant, inspiring and baffling to the end, Bowie was the greatest pop star we have seen, writes Times chief rock critic Will Hodgkinson. He taught us how to transform ourselves, to live our lives through art

There's a scene in *Ziggy Stardust and the Spiders from Mars*, DA Pennebaker's 1973 concert film on David Bowie's final concert as the leper messiah, that underlines why he was an almost religious figure to so many of us. Bowie is performing *Moonage Daydream*, but the camera keeps pulling towards a teenage girl in the audience. She's acting out her own drama to the song, singing along to the words "Keep your electric eye on me, babe" with her own eyes closed as she variously clutches her hands to her breast, raises them upwards and generally loses herself in glam-rock ecstasy. You know she's listened to the *Ziggy Stardust* album countless times in her bedroom and now here she is, in the same room as this outlandish figure in a Kansai Yamamoto silk kimono, and she's taken to another world.

More than 40 years later, Bowie's death has hit so hard that his former homes in London and Berlin have been turned into shrines. Everyone from David Cameron to Kanye West has given eulogies, and New York City has made January 20 its official

David Bowie Day. Bowie showed us how to turn and face the strange, how to transform ourselves, how to live our lives through art, or at the very least on our own terms, but he couldn't show us how to grow old. His death from cancer aged 69 on January 10, 2016, does indeed feel like a tragedy, not only because he left behind his 15-year-old daughter Lexi, his son Duncan Jones and his wife Iman, but also because he had so much more to give. Two days before he died he released the jazz-tinged, death-fixated *Blackstar*, one of the most challenging but rewarding albums of his career and his first US No 1. A week before he died, Bowie called his longterm producer Tony Visconti to say he wanted to make another album. He had known since November that the cancer was terminal, but he believed he had enough time and energy to do it.

"At that late stage, he was planning the follow-up to *Blackstar*," Visconti said. "And I was thrilled. And I thought, and he thought, that he'd have a few months at least. So the end must've been very rapid."

Bowie created worlds that others could inhabit and by doing so learn to cope with the ones they were in. When I first went to secondary school I wondered why all the most interesting girls I met there loved David Bowie so much; why, in the mid-Eighties, it was Seventies albums like *Hunky Dory, The Rise and Fall of Ziggy Stardust and the Spiders from Mars* and *Diamond Dogs* that you saw at the front of people's record collections, not *Living In A Box* by Living In A Box or whatever nonsense by men with silly hairstyles was being released at the time. "Because he understands us," one girl told me. "Because he's as confused as we are." However strange and otherworldly his personae were, Bowie was oddly relatable. His lyrics may have been hard to decode but the yearning quality of *Space Oddity, Life On Mars?, Heroes* and countless others was emotionally direct and extremely personal. He was both a part of us and from a distant galaxy that we had no chance of reaching.

He also never stopped moving, working, and developing. With *Blackstar* he pushed rock'n'roll into new territories until the very end. Like all the best Bowie albums, *Blackstar*, made with a team of New York jazz musicians while remaining within the essential structure of rock, is lyrically abstruse, but it's beginning to make a bit more sense now. The video to *Lazarus* features Bowie emerging from and returning to a coffin-like wardrobe,

while the clue to understanding *Blackstar* is in an Elvis Presley song of the same name, which features the line: "When a man sees his black star/ He knows his time, his time has come". The album finishes with *I Can't Give Everything Away*, a song that appears to be about how much Bowie will give to the public and keep to himself. It also hints towards his death. "I know something is very wrong/ The pulse returns the prodigal sons" he sings on the first verse, before concluding: "The blackout hearts, with flowered news/ With skull designs upon my shoes." Meanwhile, *Lazarus* referenced his past: in its video he wears the same outfit that features on the back of *Station to Station* (1976).

One way of understanding Bowie is to see his work as a particularly sophisticated take on musical theatre. He created one persona after another in order to play out roles that he could inhabit in public, while keeping private something of himself. Songs on his first album, *David Bowie* (1967), played around with the traditions of music hall while borrowing heavily from the style of the theatrical comic actor/songwriter Anthony Newley, the camp humour of Joe Orton and the surreal whimsy of Pink Floyd's first singer Syd Barrett on songs like *Love You till Tuesday* and *Silly Boy Blue*. Heavily influenced by the mime artist Lindsay Kemp, who would become his sometime lover, Bowie began his lifelong process of creating hyper-realised versions of himself that said something about the wider world. "I wondered if I should try and be me," he said, "or if I couldn't cope with that, it was much easier to be somebody else."

Mike Vernon was the producer of that first album. "I remember thinking, this is a really quirky record," says Vernon. "But when we did *Love You Till Tuesday* I could see that Bowie was special. I thought: if we can come up with a song which has that certain something, this guy might just go somewhere." Unfortunately, Deram, Bowie's label at the time, decided the song with that certain something was *The Laughing Gnome*, which would cause Bowie no end of embarrassment in the years to come. Today, its Pythonesque humour is rather charming.

After *Space Oddity*, Bowie's first hit, from 1969, he had a brief, atypical moment of floundering. The planet wasn't quite ready for the sight of a man in a dress, leaving his 1970 album *The Man Who Sold the World* only a minor curio at the time. It can't have been easy to combine genre-bending rock

stardom with parenthood in suburban Beckenham, where Bowie and his wife Angie lived with their son Zowie (later Duncan) at the end of the Sixties and the beginning of the Seventies, but the period gave birth to what will, for me, always be his best album. *Hunky Dory* is an existential reflection on love, mortality and parenthood, and it's the most revealing and least arch of Bowie's albums.

He tried to do his own version of Frank Sinatra's *My Way* on the heartbreaking *Life On Mars?*, tackled Nietzsche on *Oh! You Pretty Things*, paid homage to the Velvet Underground at a time when few had heard of them on the rocking *Queen Bitch* and promised to be the world's least authoritarian dad on the lovely, if undeniably maudlin, *Kooks. Hunky Dory* came out in 1971, the same year a long-haired,

floppy-hatted Bowie visited Andy Warhol's Factory and looked distinctly uneasy as he realised that, for the sophisticated, cynical New York milieu in which he found himself, long hair and hippy sentimentality was infra dig. But Bowie was a quick study.

The fact that Ziggy Stardust still looks shockingly alien today only underlines how revolutionary Bowie's creation must have seemed in 1972. Spurred on by his equally androgynous wife Angie, taking everything he had learnt about artifice from Lindsay Kemp and Andy Warhol and adding a sprinkle of rock'n'roll dirt from Iggy Pop and Lou Reed, Bowie created the world's first space-age rock star. He got the idea for Ziggy after meeting British rocker Vince Taylor,

an early user of LSD who had a breakdown and thought he was somewhere between a god and an alien, but Bowie's imagination was such that he took Taylor only as his starting point. Ziggy's one-legged body suit by Kansai Yamamoto, viciously cropped and dyed hair by the hairdresser Suzi Fussey and forehead globe by the make-up artist Pierre Laroche made the other glam rockers of the era look like a bunch of builders in lipstick by comparison. Then there are the songs on *The Rise and Fall of Ziggy Stardust and the Spiders from Mars: Soul Love* is glamorous, *Five Years* is apocalyptic and *Suffragette City* is pure excitement. *Ziggy Stardust* marked the point at which pop turned into art.

One of the remarkable things about Bowie is the way in which he used whatever was going on in

Previous page, 1974
During a TV recording of *Rebel Rebel* in Hilversum, the Netherlands. He is dressed as Halloween Jack, a swashbuckling, eye-patch-wearing evolution of Ziggy Stardust

Above, 1973
With the Spiders from Mars guitarist Mick Ronson

Right, 2000
Bowie returned to Glastonbury 29 years after first appearing, and played a set full of hits. Michael Eavis, the festival's founder, described Bowie's encore of "Heroes" as probably his "best Glastonbury moment of all time"

Far right, 1977
In Paris, in the year of his albums *Low* and *"Heroes"*

his life to artistic effect. By 1974 he had effectively fallen apart. Burnt by fame, dangerously thin, he was living in Los Angeles on a cocaine diet and hardly going out. That gave birth to another persona, the Thin White Duke, to the "plastic soul" of *Young Americans* in 1975, and to *The Man Who Fell to Earth*. Nic Roeg's film of 1976 about an alien coming to Earth to bring water to his own planet and becoming increasingly detached from reality offered just another version of Bowie.

For him to move on from there into relative anonymity in late-Seventies Berlin, live in relatively normal domesticity with Iggy Pop in a modest flat in Schöneberg and make three of the most artistically challenging albums of his career, *Low*, *"Heroes"* and *Lodger* – all of them led not by his own persona but by observations, ideas and the influence of experimental German bands such as Can and Kraftwerk – is incredible.

Bowie's influence had come home to roost by the 1980s. The entire New Romantic movement was essentially a homage to what he had done throughout the 1970s – but after 1980's superb *Scary Monsters (And Super Creeps)* he began to lose his way, chasing after either pure commerciality (*Let's Dance*) or the zeitgeist (*Black Tie White Noise*). In the last three years, however, he staged one of the most remarkable late career comebacks in modern times with *The Next Day* in 2013 and, finally, *Blackstar*. The former, possibly, and the latter, definitely, were made at a time when he knew he was dying. As Visconti, the producer of *Blackstar*, has written, "He made *Blackstar* for us, his parting gift." And he did it while staging his greatest performance piece yet: disappearing entirely. Brilliant, inspiring and baffling to the very end, David Bowie was the greatest pop star of all time.

Bowie's death has left two layers of grief. Most significantly, his children have lost a father and Iman has lost a husband. The many musicians, artists and producers he has worked with have lost a colleague and a friend. And on a wider level, those millions of us who never met Bowie, but whose lives were soundtracked by his music, who thought he would always been there, have lost someone who, in his own stylish way, helped make sense of the world. ❷

BOWIE **THE LIFE**
At his birth the midwife said, 'This child has been on Earth before'

David Bowie's obituary appeared in The Times on January 12, 2016

David Robert Jones was born in 1947 in Brixton, south London. The midwife at his birth claimed to be a clairvoyant and allegedly said: "This child has been on Earth before." His father, John, had served with the 8th Army in north Africa during the Second World War; he had a penchant for the bottle and gambling, and ran a failed piano bar before taking an administrative job with the Dr Barnardo's children's charity.

His mother, Peggy, who had a son by a previous relationship, worked as a cinema usherette and had allegedly been a supporter of Oswald Mosley's Blackshirts in the 1930s. Whether she had any influence on her son's later flirtation with fascism is not known. She did, however, reveal in a 1985 interview that, as a child, David had taken an unusual interest in her cosmetics bag, and at the age of three had daubed himself in eyeliner and face powder.

Mental illness ran in the family. Bowie's half-brother, Terry Burns, was committed to a psychiatric hospital, from which he escaped in 1985 and lay on the tracks in the path of an oncoming train. Bowie did not attend the funeral but left a wreath and a card, saying: "You've seen more things than we could imagine but all these moments will be lost, like tears washed away by the rain."

Themes of alienation were prominent in his songwriting, which he admitted was his form of therapy. "Most of my family have been to an analyst," he said. "My parents went, my brothers and sisters went and my aunts and uncles and cousins. They ended up in a much worse state. I thought I'd write my problems out."

When he was six, the family moved to the leafier suburb of Bromley, Kent, where he enjoyed a relatively comfortable lower middle-class upbringing. Although he passed the 11-plus, he opted not to attend the local grammar school. Instead he went to Bromley Technical High School, where he fell in love with the early rock'n'roll records of Little Richard and Elvis Presley.

Teaching himself to play the ukulele and tea-chest bass, he joined a skiffle group called George and the Dragons – led by George Underwood, who remained a lifelong friend despite punching Bowie in the left eye during a fight over a girl. Bowie needed a series of operations to save his sight, leaving him with a dilated pupil, which made it seem as though his eyes were different colours. By the time he left school in 1963, with an O level in art to show for his education, he had added guitar and piano to his repertoire – and then saxophone, after his half-brother had introduced him to the jazz records of John Coltrane.

He later threw himself into the bohemian world of London hippiedom, taking lessons in mime and dance from Lindsay Kemp, flirting with Buddhism, developing an interest in aliens and UFOs, and setting up an "Arts Lab" at the Three Tuns pub "deep in the heart of – God forbid – Beckenham".

Among the most theatrical of all rock stars, Bowie would adopt a string of flamboyant alter egos including his most famous creation, Ziggy Stardust, whom he described as "a cross between Nijinksy and Woolworths". When he announced the death of Ziggy from the stage at the Hammersmith Odeon in 1973, fans mourned as if it were a genuine bereavement.

More sinister was the persona he adopted three years later when, taking a line from the title song of his Station to Station album, he became the Thin White Duke: a character who had a dangerous fascination with Nazism. Describing Adolf Hitler as "one of the first rock stars", he opined that "Britain could benefit from a fascist leader" and argued that "people have always responded with greater efficiency under a regimental leadership".

In April 1976, he was detained by border police in eastern Europe and questioned about his possession of Nazi memorabilia. The following month, looking pale and emaciated due to the ravages of his cocaine addiction, he appeared to give a Nazi salute at Victoria station from an open-topped Mercedes. Together with some equally unfortunate anti-immigrant comments by Eric Clapton, his pro-fascist remarks led other musicians and grassroots activists to set up Rock Against Racism.

Forced into a hasty retreat by the outcry, he blamed his comments on the cocaine that had left him "out of my mind, totally, completely crazed". By 1977, he was carefully insisting in interviews that he was totally "apolitical" and he eschewed, for the most part – apart from a cryptic message of opposition to Scottish independence at the time of the 2014 referendum – further political comment throughout the rest of his career.

His shapeshifting as an artist was reflected, too, in the gender-bending of his personal life. There were a string of early girlfriends, including the dancer Hermione Farthingale, who was "the girl with the mousy hair" in Life On Mars?, and Mary Finnegan, to whom he was first lodger and then lover. Finnegan organised a famous music festival in a Beckenham park in 1969 at which he played. In 1970, he married the 20-year-old Angie Barnett, a brash American who grew up in Cyprus and went to a Swiss finishing school. She claimed that, on their wedding day, they had enjoyed a three-in-a-bed romp; she gave birth a year later to Bowie's son, whom they named Zowie, but is now known as the film director Duncan Jones.

Bowie had by then already posed dressed as a woman on the cover of his album The Man Who Sold the World, and in 1972 he used a Melody Maker interview to announce that he was gay. Some suspected it was a publicity stunt designed to shock prevailing moral prejudices, and he clouded the issue in later years by first confirming that he was bisexual and then issuing a quasi-denial in which he said he had always been "a closet heterosexual". Finnigan claimed that Bowie was more into women than men, and that "homosexuality with him was more opportunist and contrived".

Yet, according to Angie in her 1993 memoir, she and her husband swung both ways as "the best-known bisexual couple ever". She reported that they had both enjoyed affairs with the singer Dana Gillespie and that she had once found Bowie in bed with Mick Jagger. She also claimed he had seduced Bianca Jagger. "David made a virtual religion of slipping the Lance of Love into almost everyone around him," she wrote. "He did a lot of cavorting but I was not going to be humiliated, so I made sure I did plenty of cavorting myself," she said later.

By the mid-1970s, the couple were starting to lead separate lives, both with dangerously out-of-control drug habits, while their son was largely brought up by nannies before being sent to board at Gordonstoun. They divorced in 1980; she left with a £500,000 settlement and a ten-year gagging clause. She did not fight for custody and remained bitter towards her ex-husband, whom she accused of "poisoning" her son against her. Only days

David Bowie in 1973. Asked in 2002 how he hoped to be remembered, he said: "Nice trousers, I think I'm supposed to say. Or silly haircuts"

before Bowie's death, she gave an interview in which she claimed that listening to his music made her "nauseous". Over the years he was equally uncomplimentary about his first wife, claiming that their relationship had been like "living with a blowtorch" and that she had "as much insight into the human condition as a walnut, and a self-interest that would make Narcissus green with envy".

He married – more happily – the Somali-American model Iman Abdulmajid in 1992; his son acted as best man. Their daughter, Alexandria "Lexi" Zahra Jones, was born in 2000 and Bowie took pains to be a more dutiful father second time around. Her birth also persuaded him to give up his 60-a-day smoking habit and take up meditation. He kept his main home in New York City but also owned properties in London and Sydney.

In 1997, he became the first rock star to launch shares in his back catalogue with the "Bowie Bond", which generated him £37.5 million. *The Sunday Times* Rich List in 2015 calculated his worth at £120 million. Always a master of controlling his image and manipulating his mystique, he grew increasingly private – even reclusive – in his mature years. He refused to give interviews or promote his records and abandoned the stage; his last tour took place in 2003 and his final performance came in 2006. There were occasional guest appearances on recordings by other artists and even rarer public sightings – he was seen as a proud father in 2009 at the premiere of *Moon,* his son's debut as a film director.

Rumours emerged of further health issues after Bowie collapsed backstage in 2004 on tour in Germany and had surgery on an acutely blocked coronary artery. He was said to be enjoying the simple pleasures of being with his family; watching box sets of his favourite TV shows, which reportedly included *Downton Abbey*; and reading the novels of Martin Amis and Ian McEwan. *The Times* was his daily newspaper of choice. Most believed that he had retired from the fray for good, although his absence seemed only to enhance interest in him.

Out of the blue, in 2013, his website announced the imminent release of *The Next Day* – his first album in ten years, with at least one headline hailing it "the comeback of the century". Three years later came another flurry of unannounced activity with an off-Broadway musical and another album, *Blackstar*. Released on his 69th birthday, just two days before his death on January 10, 2016, it included a song titled *Lazarus* in which he sang: "Look up here, I'm in heaven, I've got scars that can't be seen." It seemed that he was stage managing his career right up until his final departure. The producer Tony Visconti – one of the few who knew that Bowie had received a diagnosis of cancer – wrote: "His death was no different from his life – a work of art."

Bowie reportedly turned down a CBE and a knighthood. He said his main regret was that he had never written a book. Asked how he hoped to be remembered, he said: "Nice trousers, I think I'm supposed to say. Or silly haircuts. Oh f***, don't do this to me." ❂

MY FRIEND BOWIE HANIF KUREISHI

Gossiping with Paul Smith, nipping out to buy cigarettes, 2am phone calls and trying to pen Ziggy: the Musical – the writer remembers an extraordinary friendship

Among the class pictures hanging up at Bromley Tech when I was there in the late Sixties, there was one with David Bowie who, of course, was David Jones then. And teachers used to say, "If you don't behave yourself, Kureishi, you'll end up like him."

Bowie was taught art by the guitarist Peter Frampton's father, and he taught me as well. His art room was the only place in that awful school where you could find any peace and do anything creative.

All the kids who had long hair – many of the kids who later became known as the Bromley contingent – used to hang around in that room listening to Velvet Underground or strumming guitars. Bowie was a great stimulus to us and a great influence on punk. He had moved on by then but I knew people who had seen him at the Three Tuns in Beckenham. There were photographs of him sitting there in very weird, far-out clothes – I think he was with Angie then. And then he went to London and he was gone.

Hunky Dory was probably the first Bowie album I bought – it's a masterpiece and it's so gentle and sweet. I was a Pakistani boy with long hair and velvet clothes who felt like a complete outsider – I wrote about it in *The Buddha of Suburbia*. So someone like Bowie who was also, you might say,

a freak, who wore make-up, who was outrageous, who was unafraid, was a huge inspiration.

The character of Charlie Hero in *The Buddha of Suburbia* was partly based on Billy Idol, but also on the other kids I knew who wanted to be like David Bowie, and who dressed like David Bowie. He was really a character who was an imitator of David Bowie, of which there were many. When I was writing that book I listened to a lot of Bowie because it reminded me of south London but also because it gave me courage to be an artist – to say the things I wanted to say, to be outrageous, to be challenging to oneself and to one's community.

I first met him in London with the designer Paul Smith. Paul's a friend of mine and Bowie used to like his clothes. Bowie used to complain they were a bit tight for him, although he was a very thin bloke. Bowie knew a lot about clothes. He was also a big gossip. He'd talk to Smithy about who'd been in, what George Harrison had said, blah blah blah.

I remember one very strange incident. At the time I was good friends with Paul McKenna, the hypnotist, because Tracey Scoffield, who was then my partner, had published a book by McKenna for Faber. Bowie was very keen to be hypnotised, so he came round to our house in Shepherds Bush and

Left
Reading *Viz* comic in 1990. "Bowie was a master of PR. He really knew how to be photographed"

Below left
Performing at the Beckenham Arts Lab in 1969

there was a very strange scene with Paul McKenna trying to hypnotise David Bowie to give up smoking.

Bowie had no intention of ever giving up smoking and pretended to be hypnotised. I remember at the end Bowie standing on the steps of my house saying to me, "For God's sake, Hanif, can you go and get me a packet of fags." And I said, "Yeah, all right, but why don't you walk along the road with me?" And he said, "I can't walk along the road with you. I think you know why."

I knew him really well for about three years around that time. In the early Nineties I went to his studio in Switzerland with Roger Michell, who was directing the TV series of *The Buddha of Suburbia*. Bowie came in with the soundtrack music and played it against the images. It was a nightmare for us because a lot of it really didn't fit, so one of us had to go and tell David Bowie to do it better. It was really embarrassing but I remember he said, "OK, I'm going home", and went to his house nearby and stayed up all night re-recording the music.

The next day he came in with his tapes and it was much better. And after that he went back into the studio and made a whole album, which became known as *The Buddha of Suburbia*. He was a really hard-working man.

When we were in Switzerland, Bowie would talk for hours about all kinds of stuff. Lou Reed, Andy Warhol, Ethelred the Unready – he read books on ancient British history. He talked about going around to Lou Reed's house and finding all these Andy Warhol paintings under Reed's bed and looking through them with him.

And he talked about Marc Bolan a lot too. He used to do painting and decorating with him, he told me, which I didn't know about. We sat around laughing at the idea of Bowie and Bolan coming around to do your house. He had a sort of cockney cheeky-chappie side to him. He was very glamorous, but he was also an ordinary Bromley boy.

There was a time when he wanted me to write *Ziggy Stardust* as a musical. It was very, very disturbing for me because we'd sit in his room and he'd take out the album and he'd play it, look at me, and he'd sit there with his notebook and we'd make notes on the songs. I felt really uncomfortable about the whole thing because there was this genius of pop playing me one of the greatest pop records. We talked about it for a long time but nothing came of it in the end – I think he was a bit nervous of it. He loved musical theatre and wanted to do it but he didn't know how to make it avant-garde enough.

We spent a lot of time together in those days. He was a real gentleman, really sweet – he used to come to visit my kids and bring them presents. Far from being some weirdo pop star, he was a very worked-out sort of guy.

Bowie was also a master of PR. He really knew how to be photographed, how to be dressed. And people always looked at the photographs rather than read the writing. He understood the whole idea of pop as a sort of put-on, as a fabrication, long before anybody else.

The last time I saw him was when I went down with him on the bus to the Glastonbury Festival in 2000. I remember being backstage and how cold it was. And I remember him running off the stage at the end and us all getting back on the bus and going to sleep.

He would call you at 2 o'clock in the morning and then talk interminably for an hour about some idea he'd had. And then he just disappeared. Of course, many people talk about him like that. You just didn't hear from him again, and you couldn't find him. And obviously you don't just ring up David Bowie and start hassling him. With pop stars, it's always an unequal relationship. They always have the power and I think he knew that.

For me Bowie really represents the spirit of British creativity, and everything that is beautiful and good about this country. In a sense, he was more influential than the Beatles – the way he dressed, the way he influenced everyone from Madonna to the new romantics. For his whole life he was at the centre of British pop, which is quite an extraordinary achievement. **❷**

Hanif Kureishi was talking to Shaun Phillips

BOWIE
ON FILM
A man so
eternally
inimitable,
he demanded
centre stage

With his strange, chameleon-like aura and ambiguous sexuality, Bowie was a magnet for directors, says the Times chief film critic Kate Muir

No other rock star has a filmography comparable to David Bowie's, nor such an electric presence on screen. From his feature-film debut in Nicolas Roeg's *The Man Who Fell to Earth* to Nagisa Oshima's *Merry Christmas Mr Lawrence*, Bowie was a magnet for many major – and some decidedly peculiar – directors with his strange, chameleon-like aura.

Even Martin Scorsese once employed Bowie, in a surprisingly dry and straight role as Pontius Pilate in *The Last Temptation of Christ*, taking Jesus to task for being "just another Jewish politician".

With the woozy *The Man Who Fell to Earth* in 1976, Bowie established his alien credentials, playing Thomas "Tommy" Jerome Newton, a mysterious, frail, hyper-intelligent man from another planet, with apricot-red hair and contact lenses hiding his secret. He needs no more costume than that to ooze otherness. His downfall comes when he takes to Candy Clark, gin and tonic and multiscreen television in a motel room.

In 1983, Bowie was constantly in cinemas, including in one of his wackiest and most sensual roles, making fine use of his snaggly teeth and two-tone eyes in *The Hunger*. He starred in Tony Scott's film as the (suddenly) ageing vampire John Blaylock, opposite Susan Sarandon and Catherine Deneuve.

But perhaps his best performance, which made clever play of his ambiguous sexuality, was in *Merry Christmas Mr Lawrence,* as Major Jack Celliers in a Japanese prisoner of war camp in 1942. His forbidden kiss with the captain, played by Ryuichi Sakamoto, is as surprising as it is intriguing, knocking the whole movie off kilter, right to its end with the horrific live burial in the sand.

There were lesser moments too: a short role in *Absolute Beginners*, but at least he created the wonderful title track; and Jareth, the Goblin King, in *Labyrinth*. In a perfect synchronicity of oddness, Bowie played Andy Warhol in the 1996 film *Basquiat*, and David Lynch – surely the ideal director for Bowie – used him in a cameo as the long-lost FBI agent Phillip Jeffries in *Twin Peaks: Fire Walk With Me* in 1992.

Bowie also had a self-deprecating sense of humour, voicing Lord Royal Highness in *SpongeBob SquarePants*, but his best comedy cameo is as himself in *Zoolander* (2001), where he judges a catwalk dance-off between Ben Stiller and Owen Wilson: "I believe I might be of service," he says, rising from the audience and taking off his sunglasses.

Obviously, Bowie starred in documentaries, from DA Pennebaker's early concert film *Ziggy Stardust and the Spiders from Mars* to *Cracked Actor*, made by Alan Yentob for *Omnibus* at the BBC about Bowie's coked-up *Diamond Dogs* tour. Most recently, Francis Whately's *Five Years* (2013) selected five pivotal years from the musician's life and archives.

Of course, there still is a Bowie in cinemas, in the form of his talented son Duncan Jones, who directed *Moon* and *Source Code* and is working on the forthcoming film adaptation of *World of Warcraft*. As Jones wrote on Twitter after the announcement of his father's death: "Very sorry and sad to say it's true. I'll be offline for a while. Love to all." ⊘

Left, 1969
The Bowie locks were cut to army-regulation length for a cameo role in *The Virgin Soldiers*

Right, 1983
With Ryuichi Sakamoto in *Merry Christmas Mr Lawrence*. At the end of filming Bowie treated the crew to an impromptu show

Right, 1986
Lambasted by critics on its release, Jim Henson's *Labyrinth*, starring a young Jennifer Connelly, won Bowie a new generation of fans

Left, 1976
The Man Who Fell to Earth director Nicolas Roeg was taken by Bowie from the moment he saw him in the documentary *Cracked Actor*. He said: "Almost from that moment, I couldn't believe it. I felt this was the man"

Above, 1986
With Patsy Kensit in *Absolute Beginners*. The director Julien Temple said: "Like everything he does, there was total commitment"

Right, 1996
Bowie wore Andy Warhol's own wig and glasses to play the artist in *Basquiat*

BOWIE **IN FASHION**
Dressing up is for girls. Or at least that's what people thought

Whether wearing a one-armed, one-legged leotard or the world's most spectacular jumpsuit, Bowie understood the power of dressing up.
By the Times fashion director
Anna Murphy

Men are supposed to look one way, to wear a uniform. Dressing up is for girls. Or at least that's what people thought before David Bowie. The artist formerly known as David Jones, and then, more briefly, Davie Jones, was the ultimate shapeshifter. Even his hairstyles, all 35 of them – from the early Bieber-ish comb-forward, through Ziggy Stardust's red astroturf, to the debonair Princess Di crop of more recent decades – were the subject of their own gif. What else did he teach us about men's fashion?

1

That the way you look gets you looked at...
Women learnt this lesson long ago. Maybe men thought they didn't need to: they just put on their suits and ruled the world. Bowie had an entirely new understanding of the potency of what you wear. Dress not to blend in but to be noticed and, well, you will be – that was the Bowie approach. "Off stage I'm a robot. On stage I achieve emotion. It's probably why I prefer dressing up as Ziggy to being David," he said in 1972.

He was famed, of course, for the lightning-bolt nonconformity of those early years. (Even mere mascara was, for him, a way of getting his message across – "the conveyance by which great globs of non-rock flotsam and jetsam were to be delivered", he once said.) Like no one before him, Bowie constructed a brand out of the way he dressed, only – audaciously – to switch costume, and therefore brand, overnight. He was a fashion conjuror.

Yet, in fact, throughout his life Bowie tallied with immaculately – albeit sometimes flamboyantly – executed classicism. From his 1960s mod years onwards, his default look was tailoring that bit sharper than anyone else's. In recent decades, an era in which the authority of a stupendous suit has been largely forgotten, Bowie got himself noticed by dressing like a Rat Packer, sometimes a tad amped up, always with every detail attended to. There was no athleisure for him.

2

... and that changing your look gets you looked at all over again
Every time he switched up his brand Bowie got himself looked at, talked about and listened to, and made himself richer. No surprise then that his was a model that would inspire ambitious costume-changer stars such as Madonna and Lady Gaga. No male performer has even tried to live up to his quicksilver sense of style.

3

That androgyny is cool
A world in which a woman who was once a man can be on the cover of *Vanity Fair* in a white satin body; in which men have long hair and, alas, man buns; in which fashion labels such as Gucci send indeterminately girl-boy models down the catwalk in indeterminately girl-boy clothes, owes David Bowie a lot. He beat us to it by four decades.

Below, from left
Ziggy in 1973; the Thin White Duke, 1976; 1978; 1994

Right
In Kansai Yamamoto, *Aladdin Sane* tour, 1973

4

That jumpsuits are great

Blokes outside the military haven't
cottoned on to this yet, but for
a number of seasons women
everywhere haven't been able to get
enough of Bowie's beloved jumpsuit.
Admittedly we have tended to eschew
the one-sleeve, one-leg approach, or
legs so voluminous as to suggest that
the parachute-suit theme has been
taken literally. But Bowie was right:
jumpsuits rock.

5

That colour doesn't have to be scary
Bowie's monochrome upbringing ("There
were caravan parks that looked identical
to the parks the caravans were bought
from") led him to embrace red, green, cobalt
and yellow, yellow, yellow. (From a 1970s
mustard number worn with a white and
yellow striped shirt to 1990s hot-citrus in his
Tin Machine years, by way of *Miami Vice*-
style pastel in the 1980s.) Unless, of course,
he was channelling "elegant gloom", another
favourite look, especially in his later years.
A chameleon as well as a shapeshifter then.

6

That a skinny man can be a cool man
Being thin used to be something that only
women coveted: men wanted to look like men.
Bowie changed that, embracing and playing up
to his sliver of a physique, even turning it into
part of his brand in his Thin White Duke years
in the mid-1970s (when he lived on "red peppers,
cocaine and milk"). These days skinny trousers
on skinny – and not so skinny – men, as first
popularised by Hedi Slimane at Dior Homme,
is a trend that runs and runs. Karl Lagerfeld
lost weight so he could wear said skinnies and
his now-trademark look – complete with the
monochrome tailoring and swept-back hair –
could be seen as his take on the Duke.

7

That the classics are classics for a reason
Tailoring, trench coats, trilbys, tweeds, tuxedos...
Bowie recognised that the classics had earned
their dues, and embraced them wholeheartedly,
especially, it seems, if they began with a "t".
But he also liked to subvert them, playing with
dimension – a big shoulder, a wide leg or lapel
– and colour. A particularly fabulous example
was a Union Jack frock coat abraded with
cigarette burns that he commissioned in
1997 from an up-and-coming designer called
Alexander McQueen.

Rather less dramatic was the suit he wore on
his last birthday, a single-breasted dark-grey
two-piece by the zeitgeisty New York designer
Thom Browne. It would have been a classic if
it weren't for the shrunken jacket and signature
Browne cropped trousers. Bowie wore it with
a Thin White Duke trilby and – in contrast to
those earlier poker-faced years – a broad smile.
It was the best possible summation of old Bowie
and new. A perfect last look.

Right
**At the Grammy
awards, 1975**

Below
**An all-white
Ziggy, 1973**

Right
**Colour doesn't have
to be scary: Bowie put
on his red shoes to
dance the blues on
stage in 1974**

Below
**A mod-hippy crossover,
in about 1970**

TOP 10 SONGS
The best of Bowie

Will Hodgkinson chooses the tracks that shine out from a 50-year career

1 Life On Mars?
(Hunky Dory, 1971)
Bowie intended this theatrical masterpiece to be his answer to Frank Sinatra's *My Way*, but it became so much more: the story of a girl escaping to the fantasy of the silver screen after an argument with her parents. It's an exquisite expression of youthful disillusionment.

2 Moonage Daydream
(The Rise and Fall of Ziggy Stardust and the Spiders from Mars, 1972)
Nothing evokes pure rock'n'roll excitement like Ziggy Stardust and, although you could take any song from the album that made Bowie a star the like of which the world had never seen, the third one on side A is transcendent.

3 All the Young Dudes
(Mott the Hoople single, 1972)
At the height of his powers Bowie was such a masterful songwriter that he had hits to spare and he gave this gang-like anthem to the British rock band Mott the Hoople. It's one of his simplest, too: an ode to the joys of being cool. You're never too old to sing "I'm a dude, man", while parading around the living room in your finest platform boots.

4 The Jean Genie
(Aladdin Sane, 1973)
Bowie could do sex appeal when he wanted to, and this roughed-up take on a basic Bo Diddley blues riff is a tribute to Cyrinda Foxe, Warhol superstar and Marilyn Monroe-like glamour girl of legendary allure. It's as dirty as a New York street in 1972 and just as exciting.

5 "Heroes"
("Heroes", 1977)
It may be overused now, having become obligatory accompaniment to slow-motion footage of sporting prowess, but this story of a man and a woman falling in love across the Berlin Wall is remarkably moving – stadium rock with poignancy. The German Foreign Office has even credited it with helping unify Berlin.

6 Quicksand
(Hunky Dory, 1971)
From the most personal and intimate of all Bowie albums, *Quicksand* takes on deep meaning in the light of Bowie's death. "Knowledge comes with death's release," he sings, taking on the Buddhist concept of death as an escape from suffering in a song that also references Nietzsche, Aleister Crowley and Yeats's vision of the Golden Dawn.

Above
***Blackstar* was released two days before Bowie died. His producer Tony Visconti called it his "parting gift... He always did what he wanted to do. And he wanted to do it his way and he wanted to do it the best way"**

7 Sound and Vision
(Low, 1977)
The most conventional song on the experimental *Low* is still remarkable, combining an upbeat tune with lyrics about pulling away from the world in a blue funk.

8 Let Me Sleep Beside You
(BBC session, 1969)
Bowie's pre-*Space Oddity* material has been largely written off as juvenilia, not least by himself. Yet there were some gems in there and this is one of them.

9 Young Americans
(Young Americans, 1975)
Who but Bowie could make "plastic soul" something to be proud of? With the help of black singers, including a young Luther Vandross, Bowie turned his "limey" tribute to Philadelphia soul into a bravura story about civil rights-era America.

10 I Can't Give Everything Away
(Blackstar, 2016)
Released two days before his death, *Blackstar* was Bowie's parting gesture to the world. Its final song reads as both an explanation for his many personas and a self-written eulogy. "I know something is very wrong," he sings. And it was.

Bowie's alien persona made other glam rockers look like a bunch of builders in lipstick by comparison

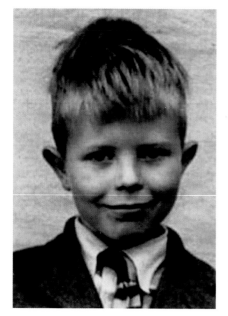

EARLY YEARS

Bowie was born David Robert Jones in 1947 in Brixton, south London, to a father who worked for Dr Barnardo's and an usherette mother. Aged six he moved to Bromley where he made his first foray into music, alongside schoolfriend George Underwood. In an argument over a girl Underwood punched Bowie, leaving him with one blue eye and one brown. In 1962 he joined his first band, the Kon-rads, but soon jumped ship to the King Bees, with whom he released his first single, Liza Jane, in 1964

Bowie spent his early childhood in Brixton, before moving to Bromley where he attended Burnt Ash School. Though his singing was deemed "adequate" by the school choir, teachers called his musical interpretations "vividly artistic" and his poise "astonishing" for a child

Above left, 1960
He passed his grammar-school exams but chose to attend the more art-orientated Bromley Tech

Left, 1968
Heavily influenced by the mime artist Lindsay Kemp, who would become his sometime lover, Bowie began his lifelong process of creating hyper-realised versions of himself that said something about the wider world

Top, 1969
Bowie with the dancer Hermione Farthingale and guitarist John Hutchinson. Farthingale became Bowie's lover and is "the girl with the mousy hair" in 1971's *Life on Mars?*

Above, 1964
After being introduced to modern jazz by his half-brother Terry, Bowie joined his first band, the Kon-rads, as a blond-quiffed saxophone player in 1962

Far left, 1962
Bowie first heard the rock'n'roll that would inspire his career on American 45s brought home by his father. Later he said that listening to Little Richard's *Tutti Frutti*, his "heart nearly burst... I had heard God"

Left, 1965
After leaving the Kon-rads and a brief fling with the King Bees, Bowie joined the Manish Boys. Here he is pictured outside BBC Television Centre, the band apparently having been barred from playing on the show *Gadzooks! It's All Happening* unless they cut their hair. The "ban" turned out to be a publicity stunt cooked up by their manager

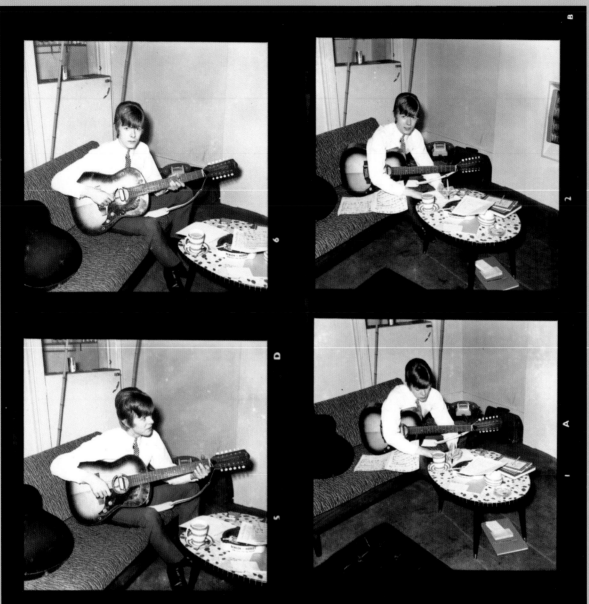

Left, 1966
It was around this time that, dissatisfied with the name Davie Jones – and to avoid confusion with Davy Jones of the Monkees – Bowie renamed himself, after the American frontiersman Jim Bowie and the knife he had popularised

Right, 1963
Photographed on Kingly Street, London, with an unnamed model for *Boyfriend* magazine

Far right, 1966
Writing lyrics on Clapham Common. A year later, Bowie released his eponymous first album, which played around with the music hall sound and was influenced by the theatrical style of the comic actor Anthony Newley

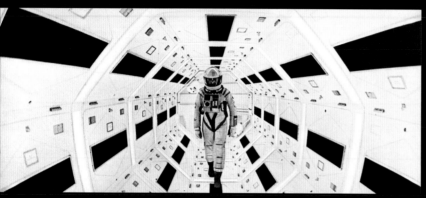

HALLO SPACEBOY 1969– 1970

Bowie achieved lift-off in 1969 with Space Oddity, which went to No 5. Released just days before Armstrong landed on the Moon, the song introduced earthlings to Bowie's first fully developed character, Major Tom

ALAN JOHNSON ON THE STARGAZING YEARS

The Beatles have been the most wonderful thing to have happened in my life musically, but Bowie came close. In 1967 I was playing in a band, the Area, and his first album came out when I was 17. Bowie wore a suit, very smart, looked like a mod; I was a mod.

He was very much ours. We'd grown up listening to every British star imitating an American accent. The Beatles started to change that but Bowie was very English, almost in a music hall sense: he was actually thought to be an impersonator of Anthony Newley in those days. Then in 1969 came *Space Oddity*; I think it was released about the same time as the film *2001: A Space Odyssey*. You listen to the production now – it wouldn't be out of place if it came out next Friday. You thought, wow! Two

years later came *Hunky Dory*, one of those albums where practically every track is a cracker. The thing about Bowie is they're always great tunes: *Changes, Life on Mars?, Oh! You Pretty Things, Space Oddity*. He could really knock out a tune.

There was also the fascination of his bisexuality. I was living on a council estate in Slough and had three kids, so unfortunately I couldn't walk around as a Bowie freak – it might look strange with a post office uniform as well [Johnson became a postman at 18]. He said this brilliant thing: that he was a closet heterosexual, which I think is fabulous. *Aladdin Sane* was the last album I bought of his. It was RIP Ziggy Stardust by then – I was still grieving. ❷

Alan Johnson MP was talking to Ed Potton

Previous pages, 1969
Bowie, pictured in Hyde Park, was influenced by Stanley Kubrick's film *2001: A Space Odyssey*

Left and right, 1970
Bowie at his flat in Haddon Hall, Beckenham, where he lived with Angie and where their son, Zowie, was born. The gothic house became a hedonistic commune and provided material for Bowie's Ziggy Stardust period

Below, 1969
Bowie's single *Space Oddity* **introduces his character Major Tom. On the same night as the Moon landing he said he'd seen an alien spacecraft landing on Southend Road**

Left

Dressed as Ziggy Stardust in a New York hotel room. The most famous of the string of personae he created in the Seventies, Ziggy was the human manifestation of a sexually and narcotically omnivorous alien

Below

On July 3, 1973, at the Hammersmith Odeon, Bowie shocked his fans with the announcement that it would be "the last show we'll ever do"

GLAM GOD 1971–1974

Extraterrestrial concerns continued to fire Bowie in his first purple period, during which he inhabited his most famous alter-ego. The hedonistic alien Ziggy Stardust bestrode the glam-rock era like a colossus

IRVINE WELSH ON

Ziggy Stardust was my initial Bowie experience, as a 13-year-old kid: myself and my friend Colin Campbell, who was my best pal and still is now, lived a couple of doors along from each other in Muirhouse, Edinburgh, and we used to watch *Top of the Pops* every Thursday. We'd been vaguely aware of Bowie, but he came on doing *Starman* with Mick Ronson. We were watching it in Colin's house and I remember the reaction of his dad, Jimmy, which was one of shock, outrage and horror. To have something that not only was really cool and strange but also upset your parents – all the boxes were ticked!

I got the Ziggy haircut and, because it was really spiked on top, I never played football at school – I didn't want to head the ball. The hard guys, who all liked Slade, would go: "Hit the ball, you poof!" This idea of androgyny and bisexuality was an amazing thing for working-class heterosexual boys. I remember Colin and me going to a Bowie night and his old man saying, "You're a pair of f***ing poofs!" and

One of my fave Bowie tracks from that time was *The Width of a Circle*, a big, swaggering, camp mystical underground song. Things like that gave me permission to get into other music: I would never have been into soul if it wasn't for Bowie, or Iggy Pop or Lou Reed; I'd never have felt comfortable going to gay nightclubs.

My second gig ever was Bowie in 1973 at the Edinburgh Empire and one of the best Bowie gigs I saw was at Murrayfield around 1978. It was pissing down with rain and Bowie came out in a white cagoule. You just thought: "How the f*** can this bastard look cool in a white cagoule?"

I never met Bowie but I stood him up twice. The first time, he was hosting the *Trainspotting* party in New York when the film was launched in America. I always wondered why I didn't go. Then, a couple of years later, I got a call saying he was doing a gig in Glasgow and he wanted to meet me for some dinner. Once again I didn't go, and I realised that it was because I thought I would turn into a 13-year-old boy again. ☻

Above
**Bowie poses with the model Lulu
for a photograph that originally
appeared in *Vogue* magazine.
Bowie repurposed it for *Pin Ups*,
a collection of Sixties cover versions
that followed hot on the heels of
Aladdin Sane. It marked the end of
Bowie's band the Spiders from Mars**

THE TIMES ARCHIVE

Bowie and Angie threw a party at the Café Royal, London, after the final Ziggy Stardust concert. Guests included Cat Stevens, Bianca Jagger, Tim Buckley, Ringo Starr, Jeff Beck and Lulu

David Bowie arrived for tea at the Dorchester wearing a bright green velvet jacket with silver lurex checks, light orange trousers, his hair dyed red, but, as he pointed out, he *was* wearing a tie, green, incredibly large, and sparkling. His face was also delicately made up.

Bowie has always been fascinated by the theatrical possibilities of pop. To watch one of his live shows is to witness a performance, not a static rendition of a series of songs. There is always a sense of occasion, highlighted by imaginative use of stage lighting always specially constructed, and underlined by the movements of his group the Spiders. It is as if the whole thing has been choreographed, with Bowie's physical height adding power to it. Until the beginning of this week he had the No 2 record in the charts: *The Jean Genie*, a rumbling rhythm and blues number carefully reminiscent of the Rolling Stones 10 years ago.

His comment on the single is: "My mother loves it." This success is the culmination of the latest part of Bowie's career, which has been split over the years into three distinct sections. If you were to play his first records now you would be hard put to recognise the voice. It sounded then like Anthony Newley in his pop period. Bowie recalls: "I always used to like Newley very much, and at that time he was the only singer who sang without an American accent. I'm not overly fond of him now... I never admired his lyrics very much."

Bowie comes from Beckenham in Kent, where he still lives, and for the first six months after he left school he joined an advertising agency as a junior visualiser, while in his spare time he played tenor saxophone in a jazz band. "Then I found myself in a rhythm and blues band, but I didn't like singing about America, I wanted to sing about my own environment."

Later he became very much part of the mid- and late-Sixties underground. "I moved to Notting Hill: living in sin, painting the ceiling blue, Swedish furniture.

I spent two years with the Lindsay Kemp Mime Company. It was flattery more than anything else that steered me in that direction. He was playing my music during an interval and expressed an interest in my writing. He said: 'If you write music for me, I'll teach you mime.'"

This then was the start of Bowie's interest in blending theatre and rock music. He appeared with multi-media groups and played only the "underground" clubs. "It's only been a year since I started playing these big concert halls." He adds: "It's very difficult to blend rock and theatre together successfully, because it always borders on the pretentious. I think Alice Cooper has probably done it very well. In the past I have used more mime than I do now. I really only use stagecraft. I'll use theatre eventually when I can successfully blend it together. I had some very interesting times with Sean Kenny about six months ago. He is very imaginative and we were doing things with laser beams. I still think he is absolutely brilliant, brilliant at lighting and his stage settings are incredible. I'd hate to lose contact with the audience. I've gone out on a limb in the past, which was satisfying for us at that moment, but by God we lost the public's interest. I love some of the so-called avant-garde things but I worry for

Left, 1972
Gender fluidity engrossed him: "The fact that there is a lot of female in a male and male in female"

Below, 1973
Signing autographs in Los Angeles

them. I think I might be taking a kind of a chance with the next album. I've fallen prey to the music of Mike Garson, a jazz pianist. He has been with me for four months. It's the first rock band he has joined.

"I find myself in a strange position. I don't know what's expected of me. I've got this glam rock thing going for me, it's a bit difficult to know what to do with it."

His first commercial hit was the plaintive *Space Oddity*, an astral theme that has affected his work ever since, although, ironically, he refused to fly 18 months ago and progresses around the world by liner and across America by Greyhound bus. It was in 1971 with the release of his *Hunky Dory* album that he pushed another of his theories forward another step. On the cover he appeared as a beautiful blond, more female than male, and that too is a theme that engrosses him: "The fact that there is a lot of female in a male and male in female." He appears on stage often seeming to dare you to guess which sex he is.

In his last album, released in 1972, *The Rise and Fall of Ziggy Stardust and the Spiders from Mars*, he produced his best work to date. The lyrics were complicated but he says he does not write hidden meanings. "They're atmospheric and it is this bizarre atmosphere, like looking at the world from the wrong end of the telescope."

It was a style he had begun on *Hunky Dory* with songs like *Andy Warhol*. "I wrote that after looking at a Marilyn Monroe picture for half an hour. I met Warhol – he's very strange. I told him all about my writing and he didn't react at all. Then I remembered he had been a shoe designer and talked about my shoes; that opened him up. I love all the apocryphal stories about him. Have you heard the one about an Andy Warhol doll? You wind it up and it does absolutely nothing."

This week Bowie boards the *Canberra* for New York. He has already become a cult there and will open at the Radio City Music Hall. "It was going to close, but rock saved it. Those poor dears the Rockettes, you couldn't see them walking the streets." ⚡

THE TIMES INTERVIEW 1973

Still glowing from the chart success of his single The Jean Genie, Bowie told Michael Wale that he feared his love of the avant garde might be alienating his audience

'I find myself in a strange position. I don't know what's expected of me'

1974
With his first wife, Angie, and their son, Zowie, in February at a press conference at the Amstel Hotel in Amsterdam. Bowie had recently finished recording his *Diamond Dogs* album; its lead single, *Rebel Rebel,* was released several days later. The album's vision of a dystopian future was inspired by George Orwell's *1984,* and Bowie had originally hoped to write a musical based on the novel. Orwell's widow, Sonia, was having none of it, however – she described the idea as "bizarre". Musical theatre's loss was glam rock's gain

YOUNG AMERICANS
1974–1975

In 1974 Bowie recorded his Young Americans album in Philadelphia, experimenting with what he called 'plastic soul' and working with musicians including a young Luther Vandross on backing vocals, Andy Newmark, the drummer with Sly and the Family Stone, and John Lennon on the single Fame. This was a period in which Bowie was, in his own words, 'out of my gourd' on cocaine for much of the time

Left and above
Bowie's skeletal appearance at this time owed much to his reported diet of cocaine, milk and red peppers. In the documentary *Cracked Actor* he twitches nervously and complains that there is a fly in his milk. In November 1974 he made an infamously wired appearance on Dick Cavett's US chat show, in which he sniffed loudly and fiddled with a cane

Overleaf
With Elizabeth Taylor in Beverly Hills. Taylor's star was waning at the time, and she was eager to be associated with bright young things such as Bowie. She asked Faye Dunaway to introduce them and a meeting was scheduled at the house of the director George Cukor. Taylor was due to appear in Cukor's forthcoming *The Blue Bird*, and wanted Bowie

to co-star. He was two hours late; Taylor was on the verge of leaving. But the photographer Terry O'Neill convinced her to stay and, when Bowie eventually arrived, he captured the pair in a series of intimate shots that have become iconic. "A pop star meeting a superstar," O'Neill told *Harper's Bazaar* in 2011. "An unlikely meeting, an intoxicating pair." Bowie didn't get the part

Even a song like Changes,
which is in essence lyrical, assumed
a threatening face

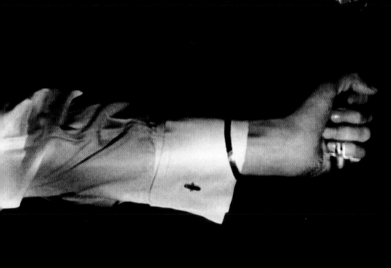

THIN WHITE DUKE
1975-1976

In 1976 Bowie adopted his last great persona, the elegantly dressed Thin White Duke, part alien, part cabaret figure, part megalomaniac. Reviewing his concert at Wembley that year, the Times critic **Clive Bennett** described a performance of diabolic intensity, deeply involved yet at one stage removed

1976
The Thin White Duke on stage in Toronto during the *Station to Station* tour

The prodigal has returned with a vengeance. The new Bowie is cleansed of glitter and greasepaint; he wears simple black trousers, black waistcoat and white shirt. His band, also, is dressed in black and white. The lighting is entirely white, varying from twin beams spotlighting Bowie's head in *Word on a Wing* to harsh neon lights for *Panic in Detroit*. The concept is literally brilliant but it would be wasted if it was not put to such startling and stunning effect.

The starkness ruthlessly underlines and heightens the tensions in each song. Even a song like *Changes*, which is in essence lyrical, assumed a threatening face. Those that are already worrying, like *Suffragette City* and *Five Years*, became physically painful.

Bowie's performance maintained a level of diabolic intensity at once deeply involved yet often seemingly at one stage removed. He went through a set of dance steps that ranged from Charleston to ballet; his arms flailed; he crouched by loudspeakers and then utilised the whole width of the stage. Not once did he touch an instrument.

The band produced an enormous energy, though the public address mix gave it a very thick textured sound. Their solo spots were frankly dull but at least they gave Bowie's voice momentary respite.

He appeared relaxed and was clearly enjoying himself right from the first number, a powerful version of the title track from his new album *Station to Station*. Everything he did during his 90 minutes on stage received a tumultuous reception. ◐

This review appeared in The Times on May 4, 1976

Left
Bowie's heavy drug use and fascination with the *Third Reich* influenced his Thin White Duke persona both on and off stage. In a 1976 interview he told the *Rolling Stone* writer (and later film director) Cameron Crowe: "I'd adore to be prime minister. And I believe very strongly in fascism... I dream of buying companies and TV stations, owning and controlling them." His salute to fans at London's Victoria station in May 1976 may or may not have been a wave

 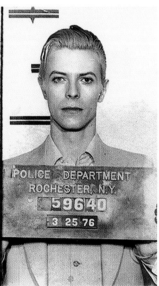

Top
Bowie with Lenny Kaye
from the Patti Smith Group
at CBGBs in New York,
April 1975

Above
Police mugshots after
a marijuana bust at a hotel
in Rochester, New York,
in March 1976

1977-1979

A spiralling cocaine habit prompted Bowie to relocate to West Berlin, where he shared a flat with Iggy Pop. The albums of the Berlin Trilogy, as it came to be known – Low, Heroes and Lodger – favoured abstraction over rock riffs, but had room for anthems too

NICK CLEGG ON THE BERLIN YEARS

© PHOTO BY SUKITA

LOST AND FOUND IN BERLIN

For me there's no doubt that the Berlin years were far and away Bowie's best period. In the time it takes for most modern superstar musicians to produce one album, Bowie produced a series of groundbreaking records.

It is difficult to think of a musician now who, having reached the level of fame Bowie had, would decide to ignore conventional wisdom, turn his back on the easy route to more money and decide to try to take his fans with him into new musical territory. It's almost impossible to think of one who would manage to do it as successfully as Bowie did.

It's the era when all of Bowie's greatest strengths seemed to reach their peak. Not just the music but his ability to find the best collaborators, his instinct for how to change his whole persona and yet still retain his identity, and his unerring knack for looking cool — the cover of *Low* with Bowie (plus orange hair) in profile has to be one of his most iconic images.

In 2012, I was lucky enough to be at the London Olympics opening ceremony where *"Heroes"* was used to spine-tingling effect. In the middle of all the live performances and pyrotechnics, Bowie's music and the video images of him were still among the most powerful moments of the night. I was crossing my fingers that we were going to get a live appearance from him and the only disappointment of the entire event for me was that it didn't happen. At that point I thought his retirement really was going to be permanent.

His 2013 comeback single, *Where Are We Now?*, seemed to be referencing the Berlin years so much. It's probably foolish to try to guess what was behind his thinking, but I wonder if it was partly his recognition that it was the period when he achieved something exceptional. ⦿

Right, 1977 Guitarist Robert Fripp, Brian Eno and Bowie at Hansa Tonstudio during the recording of *"Heroes"*. The atmospheric, now semi-derelict, studio was close to the Berlin Wall. Producer Tony Visconti recalls: "We recorded 500 feet from barbed wire, with foreign soldiers"

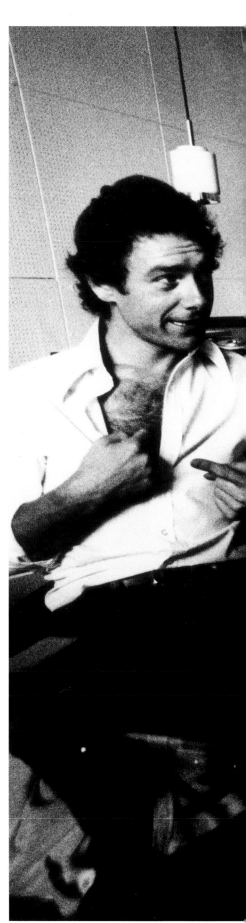

Above, 1977 Bowie and Iggy Pop collaborated on Pop's debut album, *The Idiot*, which might be seen as the beginning of Bowie's Berlin era. Iggy told *The New York Times*: "The friendship was basically that this guy salvaged me from certain professional and maybe personal annihilation – simple as that"

Right, 1977 Much of the album *Low* was intended for Nicolas Roeg's 1976 film *The Man Who Fell to Earth*, starring Bowie, but was passed up for a folkier soundtrack. When his former manager Tony Defries heard it he called it "a piece of crap" – music to Bowie's ears

LET'S DANCE

1982-83

The singles Ashes to Ashes and Fashion from 1980's Scary Monsters album had restored Bowie's commercial clout. Then he met Chic's Nile Rodgers in a New York club – and a stadium superstar was born

NILE RODGERS ON LET'S DANCE

He looked to be in good shape for a dude his age and seemed proud of it (I'd later find out he was taking boxing lessons). I walked over to Bowie and sat on the stool next to him and just started talking. Before I knew it, we'd spiralled into a passionate conversation about music.

"Damn," I said. "I had no idea you were so seriously into jazz."

"Nile, I grew up in England, where we have BBC radio," he said. "They played everything that was popular – soul, blues, jazz, R&B and rock. We don't separate the music on the radio by race or genres."

I call Bowie the Picasso of rock'n'roll (much to his embarrassment and discomfort) because of his prodigious creativity, but also because he looks sort of like Picasso drew him. Famously, one of his eyes is blue and the other grey-green. He's extremely handsome, of course, but his features are slightly unbalanced and draw you to him, with a touch of vulnerability or danger in his otherwise aristocratic mien.

[The pair arranged to record together]

Then David really threw me a curveball. "Nile, darling," he said, using a typical British expression, "I'd like you to do what you do best." His voice had a lyrical power that could mobilise me like Churchill. I thought he was talking about the two of us expanding my new experimental approach to composition. I was beaming with expectant pride – until he finished the sentence: "I want you to make hits."

rapidly. David asked me to work on some demos in Switzerland, where he lived part of the time. He picked me up at the airport in a slick Volvo model that wasn't available in the States. As we zipped along the icy roads, David confided in me.

"I'm legally blind in one eye," he said, or something to that effect. The speedometer seemed never to drop below 100km/h. I was scared s***less but his moves were pretty good.

Let's Dance was, as David described it, "a postmodern homage to the Isley Brothers' *Twist and Shout*". I knew we were in new territory and could play by different rules – rules that applied only to white rockers and maybe Miles [Davis], Prince or Michael Jackson. Now I had the freedom to venture beyond pop, into jazz territory. I was free to allow cats to improvise – on a pop single. Heaven. ⊘

Extracted by Le Freak: An Upside Down Story of Family, Disco and Destiny, by Nile Rodgers, published by Sphere

Below
With Nile Rodgers and Bernard Edwards of Chic. Bowie brought Rodgers in to funk up *Let's Dance* – it became Bowie's best-selling album

Below and previous pages Bowie took *Let's Dance* to the world in 1983 with the *Serious Moonlight* tour: 96 concerts, 15 countries, more than 2.6 million tickets sold. He would continue in the stadium pop star vein until he realised he was now appealing to the sort of people who bought Phil Collins albums. "I felt very apart from my audience"

THE TIMES INTERVIEW, 1983

'Even today I get up and think, I'm going to live this day as if it were the last day of my life'

As he prepared to return to the concert stage after a foray into film, Bowie told Lisa Robinson that his work in theatre and on screen was no giant leap from playing the rock god

His celebrated face broke into a grin. "Let's just wait and see," said David Bowie, in response to the remark that he is the one major rock star who has made a successful transition to film.

Bowie sat in the imposing pink and white Versailles Room of New York's Carlyle Hotel and seemed eager to set the record straight. In several hours' time he would make the formal announcement of his new recording contract with EMI. For the moment, however, he was intent on talking about his films, his music and his state of mind.

David Bowie has been one of the most influential performers of the past decade, creating characters that set styles around the world. But elaborate stage shows and hit albums such as *Ziggy Stardust*, *Young Americans* and *"Heroes"* were never enough. A song called *Cracked Actor*, written early in his career, may have provided a clue: an interest in mime, which he studied with Lindsay Kemp, grew into an increasing involvement with cinema (*The Man Who Fell to Earth*, *Just a Gigolo* and the as yet unreleased *The Hunger* and *Merry Christmas Mr Lawrence*) and with the theatre, where he starred on Broadway in the physically demanding play *The Elephant Man* in 1980.

The suggestion, made in an American newspaper, that Mick Jagger had expressed the opinion that Bowie had found it necessary to "forfeit" his musical career in order to achieve success in the movies brought another smile to his face.

"I suppose I put my musical career on hold for the past three years," he admitted.

"I made one album, and I would have made another last year but I didn't realise that the Oshima film [*Merry Christmas Mr Lawrence*] would come up as quickly as it did. I had just finished filming *The Hunger* and Oshima phoned to say that we were filming two weeks later in the South Pacific."

Bowie's high regard for the Japanese director, whose *Ai no korîda* caused a stir several years ago, led him to the project. He claims that his part in it was one of the most enjoyable processes he has ever gone through in film or music. "It was quite phenomenal working with a man who had that kind of versatility of mind," he said. "And generosity – it was the first time I was able to contribute in terms of dialogue or structuring a scene.

"Because of the speed we moved at, I had no vision of what the film must look like as a whole. And Tom Conti, who is also in it, couldn't get past his own role, either. You leapt from one scene straight into another – and we were doing three, four scenes a day. Oshima would set a parameter, describe the nature of a scene, state what he believed the conclusion should be and say: 'Now, what would happen?'

"Then Conti and I would say, 'Right, what would happen?' and work it out. We'd tell him we had an idea of how it would work and he would say: 'OK, we shoot, go!' – and that was it."

For Bowie, acting on film and on stage does not represent a particularly big step away from the rock-star role. He says he never felt at ease as a rock and roller, and was envious of those who really feel the part. Yet, in the early 1970s, he epitomised the role. Asked if he now feels that he used his "characters" to surmount a basic shyness and then found himself trapped by their popularity, or if it was all just a clever device to attract attention, he replies: "It's very hard to divorce the two from each other. A certain amount was 'Look at me!', but a lot of it had to do with wanting to do something very exciting on stage, a way of changing rock and roll theatre. I have a lot of pride in

Right
At the Cannes Film Festival in 1983, where *The Hunger*, Tony Scott's cult vampire movie, was screened

Overleaf
Hong Kong, the last stop on the Serious Moonlight tour

the construction of my characters and the way they were represented. It was a personal hell for me to go through, but it was a lovely thing to do with rock. It must have been great to have been in the audience. But it had very little to do with the way that I really am."

What is the way he really is?

"Quiet. Shy. Modest." These are said with just a hint of the somewhat nervous laughter which follows many of his remarks.

To have been aware of Bowie when he made his splash in the 1970s was to follow a soap opera. Looking back on the more widely publicised aspects of his personal life, Bowie now says: "I was experimenting with my emotional life. I put myself through a test of absorbing every possible experience that I could while I was young, with no realisation of what happens later, or that I was even going to be around later. It's the old adage: if I'd known I was going to live

that long, I would have looked after myself better. I can't say that I regret any of it in any way. I've learnt a lot from it."

In the mid-1970s, he says, "I just went to pieces. I wasn't pulling anything together. I came close to overdosing on drugs three times in one week. A few people told me that I'd better get out of that lifestyle.

"Then I settled down in Berlin and started my recuperation period, which took me two to three years. And even today I sometimes get up and think, 'Well, I'm going to live this day as if it were the last day of my life.' Then, about three o'clock in the afternoon, I think perhaps there is a future after all. But I don't have the kind of problems I used to have. I've learnt to relax and be my present age and my present position. I feel comfortable in my mid-thirties. It doesn't seem such an alien place to be."

Bowie, who has often said that he hates concert tours, plans a world tour beginning this spring and lasting almost six months. He says that he has readjusted to the idea. "I think I can thoroughly enjoy a tour this time. I miss it. When you consider that I haven't been on stage in Europe in six years the edge of excitement is definitely there for me.

"After doing *The Elephant Man* on Broadway, I can handle anything. It was wonderful to do a performance like that without the aid of any chemical support of any nature. With rock and roll there's always whisky or vodka or a few beers. But in *The Elephant Man* I wanted to do the six months and come out of it and remember every night. And I did."

Bowie's new LP, *Let's Dance*, has, he says, a warmth that he feels has not been evident in his music since *Young Americans* in 1975. "I wanted to come in touch with the common factor and not seem to be some sort of alien freak on the outside, which I'm not. Having travelled a lot lately, I feel more

After doing the Elephant Man on Broadway, I can handle anything

a part of everything and I want to express that feeling. I don't want to seem detached and cold, because I'm not."

Bowie may not be detached and cold these days, but there can be no doubt of the depth and extent of influence he has exerted on the new generation of electronics-based pop musicians. "It sounds presumptuous," he says, "but I really don't think about that. Right now there is a prevailing musical vocabulary that is, for the larger part, hi-tech and icy and seemingly very self-possessed. Sooner or later there's going to be a swing back to whatever is the other side of that coin. *Let's Dance* is probably the simplest album I've ever done. In fact, it was quite complex to put together, but I hope the overall impression is that it's one of the most positive, emotional, uplifting albums I've made in a long time."

Positive? Emotional? Uplifting? David Bowie? "Oh. I'm very positive. I see life as a challenge again, and a very exciting one at that."

What about all his "retirements" during the 1970s? "They were wonderful," he says, laughing. "Actually, having gone through 10 or 12 years, I see that what happens is that you get discouraged or you lose interest. Then you stop, redefine, readjust and wait until you feel the spark of enthusiasm again. What you don't know, because you're not old enough to know, is that your balance shifts. And then another kind of enthusiasm comes from a different place."

The 1983-model David Bowie seems very content. Yet how is one to be certain that this is not just another piece of role-playing?

"Ah," Bowie says, smiling. "The boy-who-cried-wolf syndrome. Well, one thing that I am sure about is that I'm not out of my gourd any more – and because I can now examine what I really think from a very sane position, and I believe that there is a thread of meaning running through my life at the moment that I have no wish to break, I think that it's all leading somewhere very fulfilling and positive. And if I feel that way, I'll make every effort to make that part of my music." ✪

CALLING OUT AROUND THE WORLD
1985

Of every artist involved in Live Aid, Bowie was the most focused on promoting the cause: he cut a song from his Wembley Stadium set to introduce a film showing dying children in famine-plagued Ethiopia. The world would see for the first time just what Live Aid was for

Above
After his performance
Bowie dropped in on
the royal box and, as
Bob Geldof talked to the
Prince of Wales, asked
the Princess: "Will we be
getting you up on stage
for the grand finale?"

Far left
A satellite link delay made
the live transatlantic duet
Bowie and Mick Jagger
had planned impossible,
so they prerecorded their
cover of *Dancing in the
Street*. It took only four
hours and the video was
shown twice at Live Aid

Left
"Only a master
showman would
understand what was
necessary," Geldof said.
"Only a totally self-
assured genius would offer
to sacrifice a song as a
nothing in the face of such
monstrosity and call the
world to attention"

TIN

MACHINE
1988–1992

After the disappointing albums Tonight and Never Let Me Down – not
to mention the critically derided Glass Spider tour – Bowie needed a new
direction. He turned towards the brutalist guitar rock of Tin Machine

Left
On stage with Tin Machine. The band was Bowie's attempt to shake off the excesses of the Glass Spider tour and return to the ranks as one of the boys in the band – albeit a singing, axe-wielding, sax-blowing one. It was, he later admitted, "a glorious mistake"

Right
With the band, from left: the bass player Tony Sales, the drummer Hunt Sales and the guitarist Reeves Gabrels. Bowie met the Sales brothers in 1977, when he joined them in Iggy Pop's backing band

DIGITAL REBOOT

This period found Bowie casting around for inspiration and finding it in such diverse places as computer games, the Meltdown arts festival and drum'n'bass culture

1993–2003

THE TIMES INTERVIEW, 1995
'My antennae have always been up for contradiction'

Bowie had spent most of his life as a fugitive from his own creations. Alan Franks found him dangerously close to being himself

There is a credibility problem here. How do you get valid answers from a man who confesses to be an awful liar and who could prove the truth of this by citing an entire career based on self-contradiction? Of course, David Bowie is not an awful liar at all, but an extremely adept one, so there is the first whopper.

The real difficulty is that whenever he comes up with the new version of himself he appears to become that thing not just in image but in substance as well, only to slough it off suddenly and go looking for the next character to inhabit. In such an ephemeral trade as his, it has proved to be a splendid wheeze. No English rock star has so masterfully killed off one persona after another in order to stay a nose in front of his own obsolescence.

Even if you suspect that this is the style of an artist who pursues form at the expense of content, you still want to know what on earth he is trying on this time.

The search has taken me to Los Angeles and the Chateau Marmont Hotel, a hill fort that looks down expensively on Sunset Strip. It is five-star cloistering. Some celebrities come here to hole up or hunker down. There goes Keanu Reeves. Others check in then speak out. For much of his life Bowie would have been in the first category, a fugitive from his own creations. Today, I am assured, he will be in the second.

On my way up to his penthouse suite, I work out that the last time I saw him in the flesh was when I was young enough to be my own son; early Seventies, at the old Kilburn State cinema. Those were the days when he used to look like an exotic bird that had flown into a freshly plastered wall. He was still trading on the otherworldliness of *Space Oddity*, and some would say he has never stopped.

After the galactic rock star of Ziggy Stardust, there was the glam rock icon (*Aladdin Sane*), the decadent Euro-toff (*Thin White Duke*), the Yuppie bopper of *Let's Dance*, the nostalgic curio of Glass Spider, the one-of-the-boys band member of Tin Machine. Those are just the public confections. In the rest of his life, you name it and he has been it: mime artist, actor, designer, writer, painter, Buddhist, critic, proto-punk, art-fancier, Weimar fascist, junkie, would-be suicide, straight, gay, ambi, neither, don't know, closet, out, married, proud father, divorce-and-tell victim, Switzerland expat and...

"With me, as for everyone, making a commitment to share your life is an epic decision, because it tempers and redefines your existence. Once you start sharing things, you open up in a much larger way yourself. I have become far more gregarious than I used to be. I like having friends in a different way than before. Iman and I recently went on a wonderful Arthurian trip in England, around the sites of Glastonbury and Tintagel. Real mists-of-Avalon stuff. It's a good myth, but groundless I suspect, because Tintagel was too late to have been Arthurian. Do you mind if I smoke?"

Nice manners, Marlboro Lights, and that south London voice. Spoken or sung, the vowels never went Midwest, as his contemporaries' did. He was always as London as Tommy Steele. This is Bromley, out of Brixton, and it brings everything back down to earth in rather a funny way, like a space suit deflating to an overall. He is wearing a shirt with a snakeskin pattern, and jeans that bag away from his tiny waist as they do on youths. There is the matter of his left eye, which is completely different from the right one. The pupil is so dilated that it looks as if it is going for total eclipse of the iris. There used to be outlandish explanations for this: it proved his alien origins, or else showed that he was able to be stoned on one side of the brain only. The truth is that when he was a teenager he was jabbed in the eye during a fight over a girl.

It is another instance of the fanciful being punctured by the mundane, and if my heart dips uncharitably as he launches off into Arthur's England, it is only because I, like you, was expecting to find something less expected than friends-and-family as the crux of mid-Nineties Bowie. Or perhaps this itself is the surprise, given all those peacock years.

One predicatble aspect of his present life is that it is not simple. There are at least three artistic reasons, and probably many more. First, he has been portraying Andy Warhol in a feature film about his friendship with fellow New York artist Jean-Michel Basquiat, who died seven years ago from a heroin overdose. On the face, or faces of it, this is good casting, since Warhol, like Bowie, delighted in manipulating images in such a way as to erode the boundaries between high and low art. Both are pop artists, although each had his origins in a different half of that definition.

Second, this year has seen him coming out as a painter. That is to say, he had his first solo exhibition, at the Kate Chertavian Gallery in Cork Street. He has been painting

I really did look at the prospect of just working as an artist until something else generated my interest

for the past 20 years and more, but says he becomes so absorbed by it that he could have seen himself doing this rather than music for a living. Rock-based pluralists in England often have a hard time from the critics, and by setting out his stall in the heart of the London art world, Bowie was asking for trouble. He never really got it, but instead received several offers for the work, including two from the Saatchi Gallery. He is a keen collector of German Expressionist and British contemporary art.

He sits on the editorial board of the magazine *Modern Painters* with such people as Grey Gowrie, Jeremy Isaacs and William Boyd. To be sure, a different planet from Ziggy Stardust. In its summer issue he has a long, meticulously researched article on the Johannesburg Biennale. An old Bowie fan – and sceptic to boot – suggested that it probably wasn't his own work, but was written for him and published under his famous name. Just one O level from Bromley Tech, he reminded me. True, but it was in art. I asked the magazine's editor, Karen Wright, who assured me the words were Bowie's own. She spoke of his "enormous zest and enthusiasm, and a complete absence of late 20th-century cynicism".

And as a painter? "Again, terrific energy.

The ultimate postmodernist approach, co-opting images from any number of different sources." She added that, because of his name, he could get access to just about anyone, and recently brought off a coup in interviewing the reclusive painter Balthus in Switzerland. In the resulting article, Balthus and Bowie share their enthusiasm for the French artist André Derain. "He was an extraordinary man," says Balthus to his approving interviewer, "because he changed his opinions every day like a cloud... you could never get hold of him really."

Third, Bowie has just completed an ambitious album with his old friend and collaborator, Brian Eno. It is the first of a planned series based on the fictional diaries of art detective Nathan Adler. The lyrics have been arrived at via a computer program that "randomises" Bowie's writing. It sounds like a shredder of sequential expression, but Bowie would not take that as a slight. He describes it as "a sort of electronic William Burroughs 'cut-ups' machine, which did in seconds what since 1973 I had been doing with scissors and glue".

The results sometimes sound like the first stab at a translation from some little-known language. I tried to rework them into conventional sense, if only to see where

After 1995's *Outside* came the drum'n'bass-inspired *Earthling*, in 1997. Bowie said he "felt free to do something which didn't have narrative to take into consideration"

Bowie had been coming from. Apart from the fact that to do that is to miss the point entirely, the software had put them beyond my reach. This, for example, from the (non-autobiographical) song *I'm Deranged*: "The clutch of life and the fist of love Over your head Big deal Salaam Be real deranged Salaam Before we reel I'm deranged."

Call me defunct, but why this when he is perfectly capable of a well-turned lyric? "I have always been drawn to the Bill Burroughs of this world, who produce a vocabulary that is not necessarily a personal one, but something that is made up of ciphers and signifiers which are regurgitated, reformed and re-accumulated. My time with Tin Machine [in 1991] decontextualised me, put me into flux as far as public perception was concerned. They didn't know what to make of me or of it. That hard-lined Apollonian thing around me had broken down, and I was once again cosmically disorganised. And this really allowed me the chance to put the bits back together."

Does this mean that he, or at least his career, needs to be fragmented like a lyric in order to make sense on some more meaningful plane?

"At the risk of sounding pompous, I guess I would align it with deconstructionism. The point made by the French in the Sixties that we are working our way towards a society that is deeply involved with hybridisation and contradictory information almost to the point where contradiction simply ceases to exist... you really feel this in America. The event horizon is so fast that there is no time to absorb properly any one thing that comes along.

"You feel it very strongly with the younger generation here. What was almost a nihilistic indifference during the Eighties was, to look at it positively, a way of adapting to a new kind of society that we had built for them. And now they have learnt how to scan the surface of things in a way it was hard for my generation to imagine. My generation wants to find a certain kind of depth between an image and a pronouncement or event. I don't think that is a priority for the younger generation. They virtually surf on chaos. They take from the top layer of life that which they need in order to survive.

"I do not want to be judgmental about this. It's just the way things are. I find I have tremendous empathy with them. My own antennae have always been up for contradiction, for two or three bits of information converging at one central point and another piece of information coming out of that."

If this is rather tricksy stuff to be hearing from a pop singer, it should be remembered that he was never one for pat answers. Simon Frith, author of *The Sociology of Rock*, once wrote that Bowie was a blank canvas on which consumers wrote their dreams. In talking to him, it becomes plain that these ambiguities of his are not merely precious to him; they are his stock in trade.

Another perceptive essayist on the subject, Dr David Buckley, addresses the notion that pop sensibilities fall into two broad categories. There is the Apollonian (reason, order, moral/political engagement) and the Dionysian (hedonism, irrationality, chaos). Paul Weller, Elvis Costello and Bob Dylan belong in the first; the Stones, Sex Pistols and Happy Mondays in the second.

The style of the first, runs the argument, is fine for everyday interaction, but successful art champions the disruptive and is fundamentally anti-meaning. Hence those Eighties performers who tried to smuggle politics into conventional song forms are less challenging figures than those, like the Cocteau Twins and the Sugarcubes, for whom a language of non-sense was the proper articulation of the self. And Bowie? His nadir, says Buckley, coincided with a lame attempt to make "useful" and emotionally engaged music in the mid-Eighties.

So, first category or second? The answer, typically, has to be that he has belonged to both in his day, and that despite a colossal success with the exuberant and uncomplicated *Let's Dance* in 1983, he is at his best when he is tampering with the rules. In the light of all this, it is once again funny to hear him performing on *Outside*, for the singing is so solid, so downright good in a conventional way. It is the kind of singing of which his own parents' generation, disdainful of just about everyone from 1963 on, except Tom Jones, might have said: "Now there's a proper voice."

When Frith remarked that Bowie had nothing to say and everything to say it with, it was not quite the insult it seemed. The fact that he has been written about as he has, with invocations of everyone from Marc Bolan to Roland Barthes, is eloquent enough. He comes from that generation of art-school rockers (John Lennon, Pete Townshend, Eric Clapton) who were never going to accept the inherited constraints of pop music. None of the other big ones has put themselves about in quite the same way and so set a precedent for the next lot. "Once you understand the tools," says Bowie, "it is quite appropriate to move from medium to medium. As long as you apply those tools in a reasonable fashion, and with a certain degree of intelligence, you shouldn't really screw up the project."

But what about the small matter of technique? I might really want to do a painting. In my mind's eye I might see every facet of a face, and yearn to

> **"**
> I have become far more gregarious than I used to be

commit that vision to canvas. And yet I know before I start that there can only be one outcome, and that that outcome will be a pizza.

"All right, if I were now to try and do a rendition of a landscape as I saw it, I would have to apply a certain amount of craft to it. But that is not the final parameter of art now. Art encompasses the idea of the idea. If you have the basic requirements to put over the idea, or a trigger to produce resonances in the viewer, then that is quite enough."

There must be limits. Without a voice, it would be quite hard to be an actor.

"You could be a mime... When André Breton said that the ultimate work of art could possibly be going out into the street and shooting into the crowd with a revolver, it suggests to me only the creation of something which was not there before. But it doesn't need to be acted out in order to get validity as a work of art.

"I get so angry when I see this huge, raging debate in Britain between the old-school traditionalists and the so-called modernists. Of all times in history, this is the one for eclecticism and for the development of a catholic taste. It is not a simple world any more, and we are not ruled by absolutes. In religion, art, politics, we are pretty played out, and there is no single system to cope with all the problems. We are going to have to take bits of the different systems that do work, cybernetic or whatever, and put them together, and that may involve a lot of trial and error. That makes absolute sense, and it always has done, since the Sixties, when we finally, finally shed that graphic American-led dream of the Fifties, in all its sterility, and vacuousness, and unsexiness. Oh, those values were so black and white."

Are they not making a comeback in America?

"I don't think that will last. It's a panic effort, the last dying cry of a system of absolutes."

Yet Newt Gingrich and his adherents

have the Sixties down as a culprit decade.

"I cannot and will not be drawn into taking the moral high ground on the Sixties or any other decade. That time had many good points. It saw the emergence of civil rights, it put the lie to a misogynistic society, and it allowed gays the freedom to manoeuvre. Equally, there were some bad things about the Fifties, like the bigotry and the intolerance, but you can't just say one was all bad and the other was all good. Again, it's this thing of absolutes that pisses me off. Artistically, that is still the climate in Britain. You still have to know your station in life."

Is he now, or has he ever been, a victim of that intolerance?

"The last thing," he says with a sudden blaze, "the very last thing I could ever think of myself as being would be as a victim of anything or anybody."

Well, he was a victim of cocaine and alcohol, although that was just about de rigueur for stars of this vintage. Not a terminal victim, it's true, but by all accounts, including his own, he was not far from that most irrevocable mode. Today he will not discuss it, preferring to spare us all another spin of the my-drugs-hell disc. And yet he was in a truly desperate state, living in Berlin in the Seventies, in the wake of a bloody split from his first wife Angie.

While he has been talking about art and detachment, it occurs to me that for that period, 18 years ago now, when he was making *Low* and *Heroes*, there was less image manufacture than at any other time, and more bleeding of his own emotional condition into some thrilling and austere music. In Bowie's case, it is ironic that there should have been the greatest complicity between life and art at the point of his own worst alienation. It is no secret that he was shocked to his foundations by the suicide of his half-brother Terry. Several of his mother's sisters had either committed suicide or were manic depressives. Perhaps it is not just professional obsolescence that

THE JUNGLE YEARS

In 1998 Bowie collaborated with Goldie on Truth, a track that appeared on the drum'n'bass artist's album Saturnz Return

Bowie said he'd heard my album *Timeless*, really wanted to get involved and loved the wild energy of drum'n'bass. It was the Antichrist to pop music in a sense, very underground.

He came to the studio in a suit jacket and overcoat, smoking profusely. He was laughing and joking, coming out with things like: "Look, it's only music, it's two things: good or bad, depending on your opinion."

He's a beast when it comes to recording. Watching him in the vocal booth, just nailing something, I was just going, "Is this real? Did I take one acid tab too many?" That guy, he's a maverick, man, beyond belief. We'd put these words on bits of paper, put them in a bag, pull them out and that was the song. It really fuelled that side of my artistry in terms of what songwriting was. When he turned up to my Metalheadz club night at the Blue Note, my mates would say, "Is that who I think it is?" And I'm like, "Yeah it's him. It's the Thin White Duke in the darkest room on the planet!" ✪

Goldie was talking to Ed Potton

---

he has been second-guessing all these years by jumping from skin to skin. Does he feel that depression is poised above him and may descend at any time?

"That's part and parcel of the artist's lot," he answers buoyantly, as a fit runner might talk about groin strain. "The currency an artist deals in is the fact and fiction of his own life... actually, I felt that the worst time was 1986, when I had to do this damned tour, and had made an album that I didn't particularly care for. Then I really did look at the prospect of just working as an artist until something else generated my interest in music, or unless it never came back and I would be expressing myself in some other form."

So what next? He will do a tour, push the album, see what happens, much as he always has. He will almost certainly end his Swiss exile and buy a house in London. His son Joe (formerly Zowie) is in his twenties and has just embarked on a philosophy doctorate. Bowie senior says he and Iman intend to start a family. One reason for his planned return to England is the strength of his three main friendships, with the musician Brian Eno, the painter Damien Hirst and the novelist Hanif Kureishi.

At this point in the conversation two people called Teddy and Paul arrive to do his hair and make-up. He gives a resigned look and apologises. They will make him exotic again, figuratively reflate the overall to a spacesuit. I have the sense of a Teddy-and-Paul as a permanent fixture at his shoulder for the past 25 years, buffing and

bouffing in dressing rooms from Brixton to Brisbane. The high talk is just beginning to sound incongruous again, but he has not quite finished yet.

"I feel I am involved in an era of tremendous excitement, because of the great pace at which things are moving. And yet we are caught in a situation of not being able to make old-fashioned, philosophically thought-out judgments. It's a sound-bite, buzz-phrase existence. If historians are having trouble rewriting history, how can the layman begin to understand it? There isn't time. It is almost as if history is ceasing to exist. And if that is so, then one presumes, metaphorically, that there is no future either; that we have truncated the past and the future into this great, fat, pregnant, chaotic, neo-Buddhistic Today.

"Now, for me that's great, because at 19 I was a Buddhist. For that 15 minutes, I had this feeling of transience, the sense that there is nothing you can set any store by in the physical and manifest world. And here we have our own, mutated form of the Buddhist Now, which we have created for ourselves. Maybe in the end it will be for the good. I am forced to be optimistic. We have no choice but to live in that Now."

I would ask him if this is a sublime piece of transference, in which he arranges the world around him as he has arranged it within him, but he has vanished. When I next see him there is a pallor that I have not seen since the Kilburn State circa 1973. There are some things that really do not change. ✪

For Bowie the Nineties was "an era of tremendous excitement, because of the great pace at which things are moving"

2000
**Bowie with his daughter,
Alexandria, at the family's
apartment overlooking
Central Park, New York.
His second wife, Iman,
was 45 when she gave
birth on August 15 at
Mount Sinai Hospital.
Having expressed regret
at his son Duncan's
irregular childhood, Bowie
was determined to be
a more attentive father
second time around and
apparently did his fair
share of nappy changing
and pushing Lexi – as
she's known – around
Manhattan in her buggy**

SOUL LOVE

Bowie's two wives were cut from very different cloth: Angie, the volatile American with whom he had an open marriage, and Iman, the serene Somali supermodel

Top left
Angie Bowie with her son Zowie (later Duncan), who was born in 1971 and inspired the song *Kooks* on *Hunky Dory*

Left
With Bianca Jagger at the "last supper" at the Cafe Royal, Piccadilly, after Bowie's final concert as Ziggy Stardust in 1973

Above
Saying goodbye to Bowie as he sets off for Paris from Victoria in 1973. The couple were married in 1970 and divorced in 1980

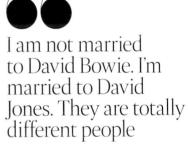

> "
I am not married to David Bowie. I'm married to David Jones. They are totally different people

Bowie married the former model Iman in 1992, after they were set up on a blind date. He popped the question twice, on the Seine (he serenaded her with the Broadway hit *April in Paris* and shortly afterwards, on stage, in French, in the same city. In 2011 Iman told the *Times Magazine*: "I am not married to David Bowie. I am married to David Jones. They are two totally different people"

BACK TO LIFE

He had gone quiet for a decade and then, in 2013 with little fanfare, a new album appeared – his best in years. Gary Kemp recalls the return of the embattled conquering hero

The first line of the first chorus of the first Bowie album in ten years said it all: "Here I am! Not quite dying!" It was like the homecoming leader suddenly appearing on the balcony of his palace. Are you listening? Damn right you are. It was a statement full of cocksure irony and swagger. The instrumentation slapped you in the face, marched you into a corner, and, with Bowie's armed guitar-gang as back-up, you weren't just listening, you were believing.

It took Odysseus a decade to return from his battles after he was thought dead, but when he did, boy did he have some stories to tell, and *The Next Day* was an album busting out with twisted tales of *chanson-noire*. What we sensed is that Bowie had visited some dark places during his time away, but he'd returned imbued with vibrancy and creative vigour. This was ten years punched into a single, cohesive statement of artistic existence. They are the stars, he says later, They're dying for you. But I hope they live for ever!

It's not an album to play at dinner parties. It demands attention. In any case, this is how my generation used to listen to albums, submerging into the two-act art form of the

Above
A photoshoot from 2013

long-player, looking for signs, not streaming it in the background of a social-networking app. This wasn't an end-of-the-pier attempt to get a career rebirth on a Saturday-night variety show: it was uncompromising, compressed musical emotion, with all the jagged, neurotic truths left on.

The sleeve, a defaced *Heroes*, stated its titular pronunciation clearly, while at the same time reminding us of one of our hero's greatest moments. Maybe this was an album full of cut-up references to the best of the Bowie canon (even an emulated snippet of *Five Years* to titillate the old believers), but it was also about the future. In a time when our new British stars seem to be made up of cruise singers and buskers, it's extraordinary that it took a man who was then 66 years old to push the boundaries of popular music.

On his return, Odysseus slayed the suitors that had risen to take his place. With 14 blows, Bowie cleared the competition. ⚡

Left
Floria Sigismondi's video for Bowie's 2013 song *The Stars (Are Out Tonight)*, the second single from *The Next Day*

Right
Bowie in 2013, on the announcement of new album *The Next Day*, his first in a decade

Top
The video for *Sue (Or in a Season of Crime)*, from the compilation album *Nothing Has Changed*

Above
Saskia de Brauw, Tilda Swinton, Bowie and Andreja Pejic in the video for *The Stars (Are Out Tonight)*

2016
**A mural in
Brixton, where
Bowie was born,
became a shrine
to the singer
when he died**

FOR THE RECORD

Glam rock, pure pop, electronic and experimental, Bowie's career had them all. Will Hodgkinson appraises the albums

David Bowie, 1967
Traditionally the shame of his legacy, Bowie's theatrical debut has whimsical charm.

Space Oddity, 1969
Featuring his breakthrough hit, this uneven collection is a foreshadowing of greatness.

The Man Who Sold the World, 1970
Heavy glam from a man in a man-dress. The first classic Bowie album.

Hunky Dory, 1971
His masterpiece. Folk, rock and musical theatre tied together by Buddhist, sexual and quasi-fascist themes.

The Rise and Fall of Ziggy Stardust and the Spiders from Mars, 1972
The leper messiah arrives. Still one of the most exciting rock albums of all time.

Pin Ups, 1973
Bowie does retro with an album of Sixties covers, only three years after the Sixties ended.

Diamond Dogs, 1974
His apocalyptic one, based in part on Orwell's *1984* and a precursor to punk.

Aladdin Sane, 1973
Ziggy goes to America as Bowie makes his on-the-road album; exciting and raw.

Young Americans, 1975
A homage to Philadelphia soul, marking a major reinvention in both music and style.

Station to Station, 1976
Paranoid from cocaine, his darkest album is a semi-religious vision of a man without a soul.

Low, 1977
The Berlin era begins. Side A features glacial new wave; Side B features avant-garde instrumentals.

"Heroes", 1977
A tribute to Berlin as a divided city, this is Bowie's most "German" album in sound and theme.

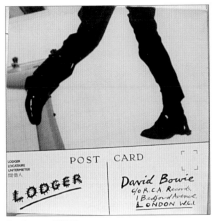

Scary Monsters (And Super Creeps), 1980
Bowie reclaims his territory from the new romantics with a harsh, vibrant classic.

Let's Dance, 1983
The superstar era begins with the most commercial of all his albums.

Tonight, 1984
Cover versions and below-par originals on this rushed effort make it one of Bowie's least satisfying.

Never Let Me Down, 1987
Intended for a theatrical show, this sees Bowie losing his way under the weight of commercial success.

Lodger, 1979
Dismissed on release, the third in the Berlin trilogy dabbles in world music and contains the camp hit *Boys Keep Swinging*.

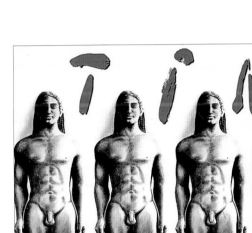

Tin Machine, 1989
Bowie forms a noisy rock band, derailing his career in the process.

Black Tie White Noise, 1993
The first of a series of albums hailed as a return to form, it began Bowie's critical reappraisal.

Outside, 1995
Returning to apocalyptic themes, this brave but unwieldy piece took on an industrial rock tone.

Earthling, 1997
Latching on to drum'n'bass was not Bowie's best move. It sounded like he was chasing after trends rather than setting them.

Tin Machine II, 1991
A glutton for punishment, he returns with his least popular project.

'Hours...', 1999
Stylistically uncertain, used in part for a video game, *Hours* is one to hide in a corner.

Heathen, 2002
Coming in the wake of 9/11, this paranoid slice of art rock repositioned Bowie as a cultural seer.

Reality, 2003
A minor addition to the canon, it contains a great cover of Jonathan Richman's *Pablo Picasso*.

The Next Day, 2013
After a decade out of view, Bowie returns in style with a rough, searing rocker.

Blackstar, 2016
Bowie turns death into an art statement with his final, jazz-tinged masterpiece.

THE READING LIST

In 2013, Bowie shared his top 100 books to accompany an exhibition on him in Toronto. It's a fascinating glimpse into the diversity of his influences

**Above
Reading David Sylvester's *Interviews with Francis Bacon* at Zurich airport in 1995**

Interviews with Francis Bacon by David Sylvester
Billy Liar by Keith Waterhouse
Room at the Top by John Braine
On Having No Head by Douglas Harding
Kafka Was the Rage by Anatole Broyard
A Clockwork Orange by Anthony Burgess
City of Night by John Rechy
The Brief Wondrous Life of Oscar Wao by Junot Díaz
Madame Bovary by Gustave Flaubert
The Iliad by Homer
As I Lay Dying by William Faulkner
Tadanori Yokoo by Tadanori Yokoo
Berlin Alexanderplatz by Alfred Döblin
Inside the Whale and Other Essays by George Orwell
Mr Norris Changes Trains by Christopher Isherwood
Hall's Dictionary of Subjects and Symbols in Art by James A Hall
David Bomberg by Richard Cork
Blast by Wyndham Lewis
Passing by Nella Larson
Beyond the Brillo Box by Arthur C Danto
The Origin of Consciousness in the Breakdown of the Bicameral Mind by Julian Jaynes

In Bluebeard's Castle by George Steiner
Hawksmoor by Peter Ackroyd
The Divided Self by RD Laing
The Stranger by Albert Camus
Infants of the Spring by Wallace Thurman
The Quest For Christa T by Christa Wolf
The Songlines by Bruce Chatwin
Nights at the Circus by Angela Carter
The Master and Margarita by Mikhail Bulgakov
The Prime of Miss Jean Brodie by Muriel Spark
Lolita by Vladimir Nabokov
Herzog by Saul Bellow
Puckoon by Spike Milligan
Black Boy by Richard Wright
The Great Gatsby by F Scott Fitzgerald
The Sailor Who Fell From Grace with the Sea by Yukio Mishima
Darkness at Noon by Arthur Koestler
The Waste Land by TS Eliot
McTeague by Frank Norris
Money by Martin Amis
The Outsider by Colin Wilson
Strange People by Frank Edwards
English Journey by JB Priestley
A Confederacy of Dunces by John Kennedy Toole
The Day of the Locust by Nathanael West

1984 by George Orwell
The Life and Times of Little Richard by Charles White
Awopbopaloobop Alopbamboom: The Golden Age of Rock by Nik Cohn
Mystery Train by Greil Marcus
Beano (comic, 1950s)
Raw (comic, 1980s)
White Noise by Don DeLillo
Sweet Soul Music: Rhythm and Blues and the Southern Dream Of Freedom by Peter Guralnick
Silence: Lectures and Writings by John Cage
Writers at Work: The Paris Review Interviews edited by Malcolm Cowley
The Sound of the City: The Rise of Rock and Roll by Charlie Gillett
Octobriana and the Russian Underground by Peter Sadecky
The Street by Ann Petry
Wonder Boys by Michael Chabon
Last Exit To Brooklyn by Hubert Selby Jr.
A People's History of the United States by Howard Zinn
The Age of American Unreason by Susan Jacoby
Metropolitan Life by Fran Lebowitz
The Coast of Utopia by Tom Stoppard
The Bridge by Hart Crane
All The Emperor's Horses by David Kidd

Fingersmith by Sarah Waters
Earthly Powers by Anthony Burgess
The 42nd Parallel by John Dos Passos
Tales of Beatnik Glory by Ed Saunders
The Bird Artist by Howard Norman
Nowhere to Run: The Story Of Soul Music by Gerri Hirshey
Before the Deluge by Otto Friedrich
Sexual Personae: Art and Decadence from Nefertiti to Emily Dickinson by Camille Paglia
The American Way of Death by Jessica Mitford
In Cold Blood by Truman Capote
Lady Chatterley's Lover by DH Lawrence
Teenage by Jon Savage
Vile Bodies by Evelyn Waugh
The Hidden Persuaders by Vance Packard
The Fire Next Time by James Baldwin
Viz (comic, early 1980s)
Private Eye (satirical magazine, 1960s-1980s)
Selected Poems by Frank O'Hara
The Trial of Henry Kissinger by Christopher Hitchens
Flaubert's Parrot by Julian Barnes
Maldodor by Comte de Lautréamont
On the Road by Jack Kerouac
Mr Wilson's Cabinet of Wonder by Lawrence Weschler
Zanoni by Edward Bulwer-Lytton
Transcendental Magic, Its Doctine and Ritual by Eliphas Lévi
The Gnostic Gospels by Elaine Pagels
The Leopard by Giuseppe Di Lampedusa
Inferno by Dante Alighieri
A Grave for a Dolphin by Alberto Denti di Pirajno
The Insult by Rupert Thomson
In Between the Sheets by Ian McEwan
A People's Tragedy by Orlando Figes
Journey Into the Whirlwind by Eugenia Ginzburg

Bowie in 1974 in the guise of Halloween Jack, the skyscraper-dwelling "cool cat" from *Diamond Dogs*

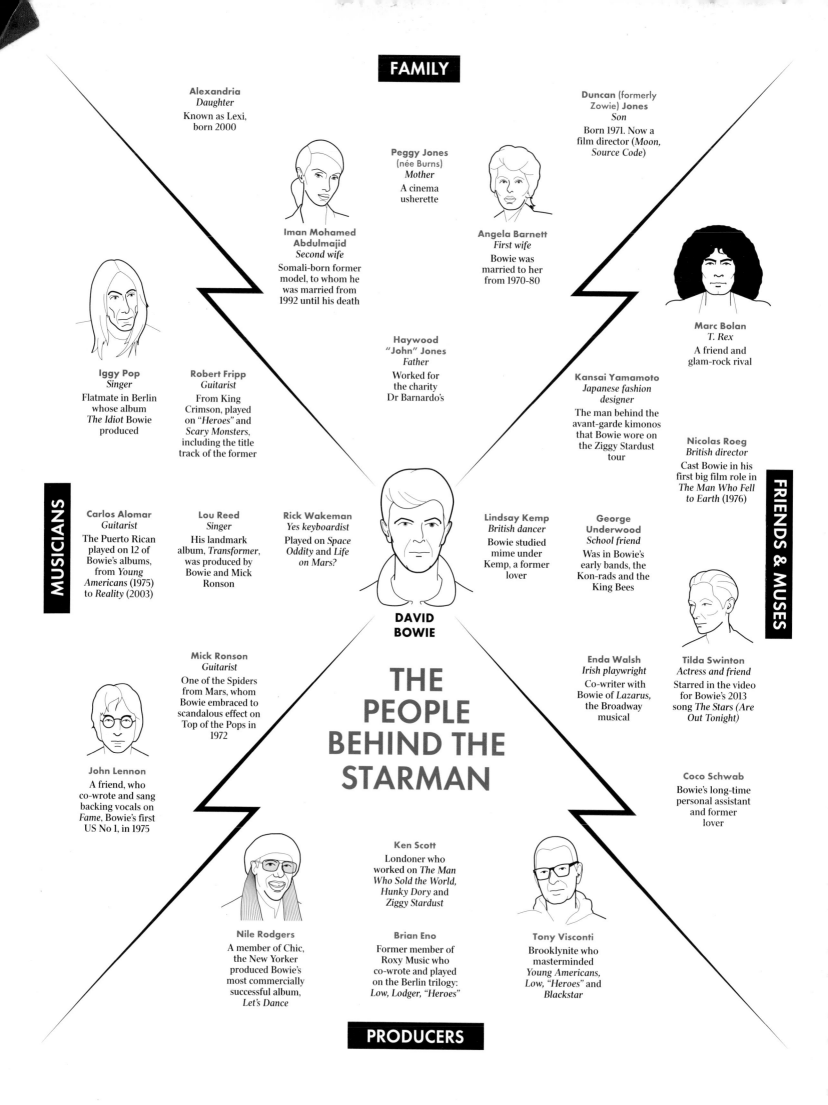

FAMILY

Alexandria
Daughter
Known as Lexi, born 2000

Peggy Jones
(née Burns)
Mother
A cinema usherette

Duncan (formerly Zowie) **Jones**
Son
Born 1971. Now a film director (*Moon, Source Code*)

Iman Mohamed Abdulmajid
Second wife
Somali-born former model, to whom he was married from 1992 until his death

Angela Barnett
First wife
Bowie was married to her from 1970-80

Haywood "John" Jones
Father
Worked for the charity Dr Barnardo's

MUSICIANS

Iggy Pop
Singer
Flatmate in Berlin whose album *The Idiot* Bowie produced

Robert Fripp
Guitarist
From King Crimson, played on "*Heroes*" and *Scary Monsters*, including the title track of the former

Carlos Alomar
Guitarist
The Puerto Rican played on 12 of Bowie's albums, from *Young Americans* (1975) to *Reality* (2003)

Lou Reed
Singer
His landmark album, *Transformer*, was produced by Bowie and Mick Ronson

Rick Wakeman
Yes keyboardist
Played on *Space Oddity* and *Life on Mars?*

Mick Ronson
Guitarist
One of the Spiders from Mars, whom Bowie embraced to scandalous effect on Top of the Pops in 1972

John Lennon
A friend, who co-wrote and sang backing vocals on *Fame*, Bowie's first US No 1, in 1975

DAVID BOWIE

THE PEOPLE BEHIND THE STARMAN

FRIENDS & MUSES

Marc Bolan
T. Rex
A friend and glam-rock rival

Kansai Yamamoto
Japanese fashion designer
The man behind the avant-garde kimonos that Bowie wore on the Ziggy Stardust tour

Nicolas Roeg
British director
Cast Bowie in his first big film role in *The Man Who Fell to Earth* (1976)

Lindsay Kemp
British dancer
Bowie studied mime under Kemp, a former lover

George Underwood
School friend
Was in Bowie's early bands, the Kon-rads and the King Bees

Enda Walsh
Irish playwright
Co-writer with Bowie of *Lazarus*, the Broadway musical

Tilda Swinton
Actress and friend
Starred in the video for Bowie's 2013 song *The Stars (Are Out Tonight)*

Coco Schwab
Bowie's long-time personal assistant and former lover

PRODUCERS

Nile Rodgers
A member of Chic, the New Yorker produced Bowie's most commercially successful album, *Let's Dance*

Ken Scott
Londoner who worked on *The Man Who Sold the World*, *Hunky Dory* and *Ziggy Stardust*

Brian Eno
Former member of Roxy Music who co-wrote and played on the Berlin trilogy: *Low, Lodger, "Heroes"*

Tony Visconti
Brooklynite who masterminded *Young Americans*, *Low*, "*Heroes*" and *Blackstar*